FUNNY
BUSINESS

FUNNY BUSINESS

CONVERSATIONS WITH WRITERS OF COMEDY

compiled and edited by
LEONARD S. MARCUS

CANDLEWICK PRESS

First edition 2009

Library of Congress Cataloging-in-Publication Data

Funny business : conversations with writers of comedy / compiled and edited by
Leonard S. Marcus. — 1st ed.
p. cm.
Includes bibliographical references.
ISBN 978-0-7636-3254-0
1. Children's stories, American — Bio-bibliography — Juvenile literature.
2. Children's stories, English — Bio-bibliography — Juvenile literature.
3. Authors, American — 20th century — Interviews — Juvenile literature.
4. Authors, English — 20th century — Interviews — Juvenile literature.
5. Humorous stories — Authorship — Juvenile literature.
6. Children's stories — Authorship — Juvenile literature.
I. Marcus, Leonard S., date. II. Title.
PS374.C454D66 2009
813'.54099282 [B] — dc22   2008024231

2 4 6 8 10 9 7 5 3 1

Printed in Singapore

This book was typeset in Giovanni.

Candlewick Press
99 Dover Street
Somerville, Massachusetts 02144

visit us at www.candlewick.com

To

Thing One

and

Thing Two:

Ha!

CONTENTS

INTRODUCTION

"If a word is misspelled in the dictionary, how would we ever know?"
— Anonymous

Laughter is one of my favorite things. It has been for as long as I can remember. One of the first books I loved when I was growing up was a treasury of "Chelm tales"—folk stories about a village of cockeyed wise men who did everything they set their minds to upside down and backward and never even noticed. Being Jewish, I enjoyed knowing that these ridiculous tales belonged to a very old Jewish tradition of humor. My parents might not always be a barrel of laughs, but my People, I was glad to know, had been making the world a funnier place for centuries.

What makes funny *funny*? A joke isn't a joke if you need to explain it. Even so, the hidden clockwork of comedy—the springs and triggers that, often despite ourselves, make us relax our serious faces and forget for a moment about boring car rides and homework and bullies—have long been considered one of the great riddles of life that people (well, *some* people) have felt challenged to unravel.

The Greek philosopher Aristotle believed we laugh at stories about people we consider beneath ourselves. (*Why did the dummy put a fir tree in his living room? He wanted to spruce up the place.*)

Humorist Will Rogers theorized, "Everything is funny as long as it is happening to somebody else."

Humor can also be a way of talking about things too hard to talk about any other way. As Woody Allen once said, "It's not that I'm afraid to die. I just don't want to be there when it happens."

The class clown is every teacher's worst nightmare and the secret hero of more than a few of the rest of us. Some of the thirteen writers you are about to hear from are themselves ex–classroom pranksters. But others are ex–model students, and most made it through their childhood and teen years at neither extreme. Some were and are outgoing people, and others were and are shy. What all thirteen have in common now is that they share a special talent for writing stories with the power to make us laugh.

E. B. White noted long ago that while "the world likes humor, . . . it decorates its serious artists with laurel, and its wags with brussels sprouts." Comedians, in other words, rarely get their due. I say, "Pass the vegetables!" Let's listen as these writers who've made it their business to make us laugh tell us how they found their funny bones, their voices, and themselves.

Judy Blume

Born 1938, Elizabeth, New Jersey

Few writers for young people have attracted more readers, or more devoted ones, than Judy Blume. Few receive more letters from their fans, many of whom write with deeply personal questions that they trust her, more than their parents or teachers, to answer honestly. Blume first won her readers' trust when, as a young mother with two small children at home, she began to write stories about some of the mysteries of growing up that had puzzled and fascinated her and her friends when they were girls and that none of the books they read then ever addressed. Divorce, money, a young person's natural curiosity about sex, and

1

the anger that siblings sometimes feel for one another were some of the unmentionable subjects that, in time, Blume not only mentioned but fearlessly explored. It seemed absurd to her that adults had ever been afraid to write about such things for children and teens. Once she began to do so herself, Blume got another, more close-up view of that same fear when some schools and libraries around the country tried to ban her books for the sake of "protecting" their children. There is, in fact, a great deal about growing up that strikes Blume as absurd. As readers we get to laugh along with her and feel passionately for her young characters as they muddle through the unlit areas of their lives, often with little more to go on than what twelve-year-old Peter in *Double Fudge* calls "stuff you know, and you don't even know how you know it."

Leonard S. Marcus: What kind of child were you?

> **Judy Blume:** I started out very shy and quiet. I can remember hiding behind my mother—having one arm around her leg and standing behind her for protection. I think I came out of my shell during the two years we lived in Miami, maybe in the fourth grade. My father, who was a dentist, was an extremely outgoing man and a great teller of jokes. He was always the emcee at his dental association meetings. My mother was just the opposite. So I seem to have started out like my mother and

wound up more like my father. It's all very mysterious how it happens. So is humor!

Q: Did you want to be an entertainer?

A: Oh, yes! As a little kid, I always wanted to be onstage. I wanted to be a movie star. I was funny, and I liked being funny. During the two "Sally Freedman" years, when we were living in Miami, I remember getting all the kids in the apartment house together to do a "production"—a show for the parents who lived there. I made all the posters and playbills, which said, "Starring Judy Sussman, with . . ."—just the way they did it in the movies. In fifth grade, I did another big production, this time at school. I starred, I dressed everybody, and we even had a little band. I liked producing. I had a school chum, who is still my best friend. In high school, the two of us thought we were so witty, so full of what we were then allowed to call "gay repartee."

Q: Did you enjoy writing then?

A: We had so little creative writing in the Elizabeth, New Jersey, public schools that I attended. I don't think we were ever asked to write a story, which is sad. On the other hand, I didn't have anyone pulling apart my writing, either. In high school I wrote for the newspaper.

I really started to write as a student in an extension course at NYU. I had graduated from NYU a few years earlier and had received a brochure about the course in the mail. By then I was married, had two small children, and was living in New Jersey. We were a very small group. I loved the experience, and I loved our teacher, even though she had a lot of rules for us about the things you weren't supposed to write about in a children's book. I wrote *Iggie's House* in that class. When the course ended, I signed up for it again.

Q: So your idea about writing was always to write for young people?

A: I never thought about anything else. I was maybe twenty-six years old, but I still saw the world through the eyes of a child. My life experiences at the time weren't anything compared to my childhood experiences and thoughts and feelings.

Q: Once you began to write, what future did you imagine for yourself? What was your dream?

A: It was a pretty basic dream: *Oh, please, please, please someday let me be published!* Like Margaret, what I really thought was, *Please, God!* Then once I had been published, the dream became, *Please, God, let somebody* read *this stuff.* You get greedier and greedier!

Q: Were you reading children's books by other writers for inspiration?

A: I would go to the public library and come home with armloads of books. I would read these books, or read until I didn't want to read anymore, and then I would divide them into piles. There were the boring books, the "I do not want to write books like these" pile. And then there was the "These books are so good" pile. I literally fell off the sofa laughing while reading Beverly Cleary. I thought her books were so funny and so wonderful. Elaine Konigsburg had just published *Jennifer, Hecate, Blah-Blah-Blah, and Elizabeth*—that impossible, wonderful title. I loved that book. There was a candy factory near where we lived that my little babies and I would pass every day on our way to the supermarket or the gas station. There's a description of a similar factory in *Jennifer, Hecate*—about how good a candy factory smells. The one we passed was just like it.

Q: Can you recall the first time you saw one of your books on a store shelf?

A: I remember finding *Margaret* shelved with the Bibles. *That* was funny! I said to the woman in the store, "That book doesn't belong with the Bibles." She said, "Yes, it does." I said, "No, I don't think so." She said, "Well, listen to this," and read to me from the jacket copy, but she read it wrong. She read, "Margaret Simon: twelve chats with God." Of course what it *did* say was, "Margaret Simon, twelve, chats with God." "You see," she said, "that is why this book certainly *does* belong with the Bibles." There was nothing I could do to convince her otherwise.

Q: Do you ever still look for your books?

A: Have I ever walked into a bookstore and *not* looked for my own books? I'm ashamed to tell you, *of course* I look for my own books. It's always exciting to find your book. It's still exciting. I love it. When my kids were young, they used to go into a bookstore and would turn my books out on the shelves. They would do it, and they'd run out!

Q: Is Fudge one of your favorite characters?

A: He has to be, because he brought me so many readers, and because he's based on my son Larry. Fudge is thirty-five now. Larry is forty-four. So it's a long time ago that he was Fudge-like. But we met a little boy the other evening whose father reads him Fudge every night. We were at this boy's grandma's house, having dinner. His father said to him, "Do you know who this is? This is Judy Blume, who writes the Fudge books." The little boy's mouth just dropped, and then he came over to me and kind of petted my arm. Then I said, "And guess who this is?" pointing across the table to Larry. Larry said, "I was Fudge." The little boy just couldn't believe it. He said, "Oh!" and now he calls Larry "Fudge." Yes, Fudge is special in the way that Margaret is special.

Q: How did you get started on the Fudge books?

A: Fudge was just for fun, to be entertaining. I remember that when Larry was maybe in fourth grade, he would go to bed with one of the Great Brain books [by John D. Fitzgerald], and I would hear him laughing and laughing his head off, and I would think, *This is the most wonderful thing in the world.*

Tales of a Fourth Grade Nothing was going to be a picture book. I had written just the final chapter, the one in which Fudge swallows the turtle. Nobody would publish it. I saved the rejection letters, which said wonderful things like, "This is very funny, but it teaches small boys to swallow turtles" and "This is very funny but it could never happen." Then an editor took me to lunch and suggested I write a longer book about the characters. That summer, it just came out of me. Usually, I'm a big rewriter. But I wrote that book in maybe six weeks, without rewriting at all. The editor loved it and published it exactly as it was.

The Fudge books are episodic. I like to write that way. You put your characters in a situation and see what they'll say and do versus what they're thinking inside. Funny things aren't things that I think about. Humor comes out spontaneously,

Judy Blume at summer camp, age fourteen

and it either comes or it doesn't come. That may make writing funny books harder. But when it does work, it's a fun day at the computer or the yellow pad.

Q: In *Blubber* you show a cruel side of laughter, when it's used as a weapon to single out someone from the group.

A: Lots of kids do that. I corresponded for a while with a fifth-grade teacher who told me that he started out every school year by reading *Blubber* aloud to the kids, and that it set a tone of kindness within his classroom. He said that when he started the reading, there would always be hysterical laughter, because at first they thought it was really funny. And then, all of a sudden, it was *wham*! They got it, and there was dead silence, because they all realized that any one of them could be in this position or could do those awful things. Adults say, "I want to protect my children from that." But they're not there with their children in school every day. The best way to protect them is to talk about things. A teacher has to be brave to read that book out loud. I think most teachers now would be afraid to.

Q: In *Otherwise Known as Sheila the Great,* Sheila says, "Then I tried lying on my back. I looked up at the ceiling. I tried to think of something funny. Something that would give me a good dream." Humor for her is a way of coping with fear.

A: Sheila is so scared of everything. I was too when I was a kid. I gave Sheila some of my childhood fears.

Q: You once said that as a child you hated secrets, and that you still do.

A: I like to know everything. My husband says that's being nosy. But it's not nosy. It's being extremely curious. As a kid, adults kept secrets that no one would tell me! Secrets about family members, neighbor secrets. When I look back now, I think, *Why shouldn't they have kept secrets?* But the trick is not to let children know that secrets are being kept. And of course children are very, very good at knowing.

Q: Louise Fitzhugh's heroine Harriet becomes a spy to find out everyone's secrets. What did you do?

A: When adults didn't tell me what I wanted to know, I invented. And because I was a worrier, what I invented was much worse than the truth. I wanted to know about sex, of course, and nobody talked to me about that. On the other hand, I never came out and said to my parents, "Guess what? I want to know about sex." I couldn't have said that either. So how would they have known I wanted to know? They probably didn't. I've advised many children, "Why don't you write your parents a letter just like the one you wrote to me?"

Q: Have the letters you receive from readers changed much over the years?

A: I get mostly e-mail now. I like e-mail, because it's so immediate. But I don't think that even kids pour out their hearts in e-mail in the same way that they did when they sat down with paper and pencil. Then again, kids have a lot of other places they can go now to find out the things they want to know on their own. They have the Web.

I've received a million letters in the last few years—there must be some real effort going on—about *Superfudge,* and the chapter called "Santa Who?" in which Fudge says, "I know there's no Santa. . . . Mommy and Daddy think I believe in him . . . so I pretend." I've been told I've ruined Christmas forever. Talk about no sense of humor! The censors want things ordered in their own way, and they want to give the orders. I think that adults have always been a little bit nervous about books that kids like, or anything that kids really like. If a kid likes it, there must be something wrong with it. Not all adults, of course. I always think it's great when you can laugh with your kids. What could be better?

Q: Do you ever make yourself laugh while you are writing?

A: Oh, yes. Laugh—and cry.

all three of us blew at once. Dylan's pussy willow flew out again and landed on
the other side of our line. Justin's came out but it just dropped to the ground and
lay there next to his foot. I blew and blew but nothing happened.

"Try again," Dylan said. ~~"Hold your other nostril closed and blow as hard
as you can."~~

So I did. But nothing happened.

"Let me look," Justin said. He looked up my nose, then shook his head. "I
don't see anything. Are you *sure* it didn't come out?"

"I can feel it," I ~~said~~ to him. "It's like having a big, furry booger up my nose."
~~Dylan and Justin laughed. But I didn't.~~ Justin said, "Get your magnifying
glass, Jake."

"Can't," I told him. "I gave it to my sister."

"Why'd you do that?" Dylan asked.

I couldn't tell them it was a mistake. I couldn't say I wished I could take it
back. That once you give somebody a present, it's going, going, gone!

Justin said, "Go ask your sister if we can borrow it."

"You come with me," I said.

So the three of us went inside and up to the Great One's room. She was at
her desk, cutting pictures out of a magazine. "What are you doing?" I asked.

Manuscript page from *Going, Going, Gone! with the Pain & the Great One*

Q: Do you read your work aloud as you write it?

A: Not while I'm writing it. But I certainly do once I have stuff on paper. It's the best advice that I could give to anybody who wants to write, especially when you're doing humor, which is so much about timing and so much about voice. You can tell a story in a million ways. You have to be able to hear it. You have to be able to hear the characters talk. Every time I start a new book, I have to find the voice. When I was starting *Wifey*, it took me three months to find it.

Q: Do you keep to a work schedule?

A: Yes. I'm sitting here now struggling to get a first draft done of the third book about the Pain and the Great One before Labor Day. Time is running out. When I'm writing a book, it's every day, seven days, if I can. I get up, get dressed, have breakfast, and pretend that I'm going out to work. I'm in this little cabin for three hours in the morning. Nasty weather's good for me, because when it's beautiful out I want to go kayaking. That's how I've always worked. If I don't do it first thing, then I'll never do it that day. I still get my best ideas with a pencil in my hand, scribbling on the printout.

Q: Does having written so many books make it any easier for you now?

A: No, it makes it worse. It's so much harder to be fresh and funny and new when you've done it twenty-something times. When I started, there was so much stuff that wanted to come out, that needed to come out.

The books I'm writing now are really books of short stories. I've never been a short-story writer, and for me that's hard. I like this brother and sister. Jake's a little Fudge-like but a lot more real. Four books, seven stories each: I thought, *It's now or never, Judy!* I wrote several stories before I signed a contract, just to make sure I could do it. I'm writing probably the third draft of a story now, and I have to get it right.

I do understand much more about the process than I did when I was starting out. This morning, I fell asleep at my computer, even though I wasn't tired—and I knew that that was telling me something. Walk away from it today, and when you come back to it tomorrow, it's going to be OK. It's going to come to you. If there's a problem within a story, I may think about that while I'm taking my morning walk.

Q: Tell me more about how you revise a book.

A: I'm not an outliner, though I'm not going into it cold, either. I have little notes and scribbles. Sometimes things happen while I'm writing that delight me. There are more good days on later drafts than there are on early drafts. During a first draft, most days are not good days at all. But then there are great days. I had a day last week when a story I was writing just came together.

Q: How many drafts might there be?

A: Oh, many. Many, many, many, many. I keep all the drafts rather than throwing them away, so that I can actually see how many drafts I'm going through. Sometimes it's twenty-something.

Q: What do you like best about being a writer?

A: I like the creative high. I like inventing characters. At this point in my career, I like the freedom to make my own schedule. Sometimes I like locking myself up in my little cabin, and sometimes when I think I hate it and I don't do it for a while, I find that I miss it. Then I go back in there again to be by myself and write some more.

A JUDY BLUME READER

Are You There God? It's Me, Margaret. (Bradbury, 1970)
Blubber (Bradbury, 1974)
Deenie (Bradbury, 1973)

The Fudge books:
    Tales of a Fourth Grade Nothing (Dutton, 1972)
    Otherwise Known as Sheila the Great (Dutton, 1972)
    Superfudge (Dutton, 1980)
    Fudge-a-Mania (Dutton, 1990)
    Double Fudge (Dutton, 2002)

Here's to You, Rachel Robinson (Orchard, 1993)

The Pain & the Great One books:
    Soupy Saturdays with the Pain & the Great One,
        illustrated by James Stevenson (Delacorte, 2007)
    Cool Zone with the Pain & the Great One, illustrated
        by James Stevenson (Delacorte, 2008)
    Going, Going, Gone! with the Pain & the Great One,
        illustrated by James Stevenson (Delacorte, 2008)

Starring Sally J. Freedman as Herself (Bradbury, 1977)

BEVERLY CLEARY

Born 1916, McMinnville, Oregon

S it here for the present," a teacher tells a new kindergartner at the start of the day. Story time comes and goes,
and then the children file out the door for recess—
all but that one kindergartner, Ramona, who remains firmly
planted in her place. When the teacher asks her what the
matter is, Ramona explains, "You told me to sit here for the
present, and I have been sitting here ever since school started
and you haven't given me a present. . . . Words," Ramona
decides that day, are "so puzzling." Words—and life, too.
Like Ramona, Beverly Cleary decided long ago that life is
not just puzzling but "humorous, sorrowful, and filled with
problems that have no solutions."

Cleary grew up in Oregon, first on a farm in Yamhill and then on Klickitat Street in Portland, in a neighborhood much like the one where so many of her stories take place. After college, she enrolled in library school and went to work at the public library in Yakima, Washington. She was assigned for a time to a bookmobile, an experience she especially liked because it meant bringing books to farm children who might not otherwise have had access to any. Cleary was still a librarian when, at age thirty-three, she published her own first book, *Henry Huggins.*

A short, round-faced woman with an owlish gaze, Cleary is one of America's most honored writers. Her many awards include the Newbery Medal for *Dear Mr. Henshaw.* A public garden and fountain in Portland featuring sculptures of Ramona, Henry Huggins, and Ribsy celebrate her lifework. A woman of strong convictions, she believes that people who think that humorous books aren't as good as "serious" ones have got it backward. As *Dear Mr. Henshaw's* Leigh Botts says, "A book doesn't have to be funny to be good, although it often helps."

Leonard S. Marcus: What kind of child were you?

    Beverly Cleary: I was an only child, and when we lived on the farm I lived in great freedom and isolation. I wanted more than anything to have someone to play with. Then we moved to Portland, and school came as a terrible shock to me, as it does for Ellen in *Ellen Tebbits*, which is my most autobiographical novel as far as feelings go. I had a miserable time in the first grade, because I now found that I had to be very much concerned about how I should behave and what I was supposed to do. Like Ellen, I had a terrible time trying to hide my underwear at a ballet class, and I rode a horse that went out into the middle of a stream and just stood there. But *Ellen Tebbits* is autobiographical as to feelings even more than it is as to actual events.

Q: **You've said that while you were still living in Yamhill, you were more like Ramona than Ellen.**

A: Yes, but even in Portland I had Ramona thoughts in the back of my mind!

Q: **Did being an only child have something to do with your becoming such an acute observer of people?**

A: In first grade I had a very strict teacher who would hit her students on the hand with a metal-tipped bamboo pointer. Because I didn't know how to behave, I kept still and observed so that I wouldn't do anything terrible that would bring down the wrath of this teacher on me. Poor woman! In those days there were forty pupils in a class, and none of us had gone to kindergarten. She had to be strict.

But I think that observing must be genetic. My son is very observant. When he was in college and didn't know what direction he wanted to go in, he took a three-day aptitude test. He was told that he was unusually observant and that he should be a gambler or a detective. I didn't raise my son to be a gambler!

Beverly Cleary, age six, shortly before her family moved to Portland

Q: Did he become a detective?

A: No, he didn't. But now my grandson is very observant.

Q: Stories for young people are usually about characters of the same age as the reader, or else a bit older. Your Ramona books don't follow that pattern.

A: At first, I didn't think I could write a book about Ramona, because I had not gone to kindergarten myself. But in due time I had a pair of kindergartners at home and learned more about the stresses of kindergarten. A few years after that, I noticed that my children had begun to feel that the things they had done in kindergarten were hilarious. And it was then that I was able to write the book.

Q: What else did you learn from your children that helped you?

A: Having twins was a great advantage for a writer, because they were always put in different classes at school and at the dinner table they would compare notes on what went on in their classrooms.

Q: How did growing up during the Great Depression affect your life?

A: My father was a son of pioneers, and my generation was brought up on pioneer values: "Stand on your own two feet"— which I have done as best I could. Pioneers never asked for help, but they helped others when they saw it was needed. Selling the farm was really a terrible decision for my father to have to make. The farm hadn't failed. It was the economy that failed. But I think he always had feelings of guilt that he had sold his heritage. My mother read me Maeterlinck's *The Blue*

Bird, and when she came to the end, she said, "It's true. You find happiness in your own backyard."

Q: Ramona and so many of your other characters do just that.

A: I didn't particularly think about it. I wrote about the neighborhood I knew when I was growing up. I didn't go off alone until I was in the seventh or eighth grade and having my teeth straightened. Then I started going "overtown," as we would say because we went over the river to town.

Q: One of the basic facts of Ramona's life is that her family doesn't have much money.

A: I've had so many grateful letters from children saying they liked the books because Ramona didn't have enough money. I think really that most children don't.

Q: There's that touching—and very funny—scene at the end of *Ramona Quimby, Age 8,* when the Quimbys are coming home from a restaurant. A stranger at the restaurant has just complimented them, saying they look like a "happy family." A moment earlier, the Quimbys wouldn't have said this about themselves. But now they decide that perhaps they *are* a happy family.

A: That was a little bit autobiographical. Once when our children were four—four's a pretty difficult age—and it had been a horrible, rainy day, I was practically tearing my hair out at the roots, so we decided we would go out to dinner. We went to a Mexican restaurant that the children liked because there were so many things around to look at. When it was time to go, we found that an elderly gentleman had paid for our dinners because we were "such a nice family." We *tried* to be nice after that.

Q: When you were a young girl, your mother suggested that you write a book review for a contest sponsored by a local newspaper. Was your winning review your first publication?

A: Yes. After that, I was a celebrity. My picture in the paper was about one inch square.

Q: Did you feel encouraged to keep writing?

A: Perhaps. I don't know. I just took every opportunity that came along. I wrote a letter to the Shopping News that was published and for which I was paid a dollar. I learned a valuable lesson when the Keds shoe people sponsored a local contest for the best essay about an animal. I wrote mine, about the beaver, on little three-inch-square pieces of paper. And I won—because nobody else had entered the contest. That was a great lesson. Sometimes you're way ahead by just trying. I won another contest that nobody else entered by making a block print for the cover of a Camp Fire Girls publication. It wasn't a very good print, but I got five dollars for that!

Q: Your seventh-grade teacher, Miss Smith, made a point of encouraging your writing, didn't she?

A: I felt a great sense of freedom with Miss Smith. She and a Miss Harrington, who taught Auditorium—a strange name for a course about public speaking—were the first teachers who

Ramona's troubles seemed to vanish. She had taught her baby sister to stick out her tongue.

Ramona's World

ever encouraged any creativity. Until they came along, the purpose of education had been uniformity. Miss Smith saw to it that I was in plays and things. But I think the idea to write was there earlier. I remember that in the third grade I wrote a little story, also on three-inch-square pieces of paper, took it to school, and showed it to the teacher, who read it to the class. Then the girl who was allegedly my best friend said I had gotten it out of a book. Well, I *hadn't* gotten it out of a book. It was a sort of fairy tale, and I was a great reader of fairy tales, so that probably my "literary source" was Joseph Jacobs's *More English Fairy Tales,* or some such collection. I was quite crushed that my best friend would accuse me of such a thing.

Even without Miss Smith's encouragement, I think I would have gone in the direction of becoming a writer, because children are well known to live out their parents' frustrations, and my mother always said she wanted to write. I don't know why she didn't. Her letters were lively, as were her accounts of whatever was going on in the neighborhood, and she had a great sense of humor—about anything except herself, and me. I was expected to be perfect. My mother was a small, intense woman who was frustrated by her life as a housewife in those days when married women were expected to stay at home. She had been a teacher and loved teaching. She loved Latin and insisted I study it. After two years I balked and insisted on taking French. Today I wish I had studied more Latin.

Q: In the Ramona books, Beezus worries about not having enough imagination.

A: Many children feel that way. I question teachers who expect children to write stories. I get desperate letters from children saying, "I can start a story but I never can finish it." I think teachers would be wiser to teach children to listen and to write a page of dialogue. There are lots of good subjects, such as a quarrel between a brother and sister, that they would really like to write about. A description of something they like or don't like. A description of a cafeteria lunch, for example, might set off some creative ideas.

Q: How did you go about getting your first book published?

A: I was working at the Sather Gate Bookshop, in Berkeley, as Christmas help when the editor of Morrow Junior Books, Elisabeth Hamilton, came out to the University of California to speak. She had the reputation of being the smartest editor in the business. I listened to her, and I liked the idea of being able to see the person to whom my manuscript would go. At the end of six weeks, she accepted *Henry Huggins*.

Elisabeth was a tall, handsome woman with a strong personality. Communication with her was usually by letter. But after my second manuscript, *Ellen Tebbits*, had been accepted, she came out to California again to speak at the university and, this time, to see me, too. She made it quite clear that she wanted to see me in my home. I think she wanted to know what sort of people we were, how we lived. So I invited her to dinner in fear and trembling.

We had a very charming little redwood house in the Berkeley hills, with eucalyptus trees, on the side of a canyon. The house had come with a cat that we dearly loved. I remember that Elisabeth didn't eat dessert. I had slaved over that dessert!

Elisabeth sent me a telegram when she first read the manuscript of *Fifteen*, which was a big departure for me, a book for teenage girls. I was in the dentist's chair, and my husband read the telegram to me over the telephone. I believe she said that it was the best book I had ever written. I burst into tears, and the dentist looked at me and said, "Isn't that *good* news?" *Fifteen* was a little triumph for me, because when I had told Elisabeth that some junior-high-school girls had asked me to write a book "like you write, only for our age," I had said I thought I would. And she had said, "Well, you can if you want. But it won't sell the way your others do." Well, it *really* took off and sold far better than the others.

Q: Years later, *The Mouse and the Motorcycle* was another departure—your first fantasy.

A: I was ready to do something different. At the time I wrote *Fifteen*, I just couldn't see going on writing about Henry Huggins forever. The inspiration for *The Mouse and the Motorcycle* came from a trip we took to England when our children were nine years old and our son was ill. We were staying in a spooky old hotel and bought him some miniature toys for while he had to stay in bed. One of those toys was a little motorcycle. And when we came home, a neighbor showed me a mouse that had fallen into a bucket in her garden, and the thought crossed my mind that that mouse was just the right size to ride the motorcycle. I mentioned the possibility of a motorcycle-riding mouse at dinner, and both children said, "Oh, write it!" I wrote it very fast, because every day when they came home from school, they wanted to know what Ralph had done.

I was very pleased with the film adaptation of that book, and I keep the model of Ralph used for the film, or one of him, in a bell jar on my bedside table. It's larger than a real mouse, and it's actually ermine dyed with Lady Clairol and has enough machinery in it to fly a DC-10!

Q: Do you have a work routine?

A: That has changed over the years. I used to think my stories out quite carefully before I wrote a word. That was a result of my training as a storyteller in the library. I mentally told my stories and then wrote them down. But now I don't do that, and I find I'm a rather disorganized writer. I know the character and the incident I'm describing and not much else. I write about three times as much as I need to, and then I cut. I've decided I don't like to write but I love to revise. It's great fun to cut and slash and rearrange. I don't necessarily begin at the beginning of a book. For years, I started my books on January second, and they were all usually finished, accepted, and edited by June. Then I'd think about something else until the next January.

Q: Do you consider yourself a perfectionist?

A: I'm a perfectionist in sewing and writing, but not in other things. I'm always at war with my typewriter. My typing grows worse with every passing year.

Q: You say in *My Own Two Feet* that you like to write when it's raining.

A: I suppose I feel a little more shut in when it's raining. Also, rain is always a soothing sound to me, having grown up in Oregon.

Q: Humorous writing doesn't always get quite the same respect that "serious" writing does. What are your thoughts about that?

> **A:** I think that books that have humor are the very best ones! I once had a teacher write me about *Ramona the Pest* and ask, "Are you *perhaps* writing satire?" I think that perhaps I am, but I don't do it intentionally. It just comes out that way. It was children who told me that my books were "funny and sad." I think that that is my view of life, that life is funny *and* sad.

Q: There's a funny moment in one of the Ramona books when the father announces that he's studying child psychology and Ramona is appalled.

> **A:** Ramona feels entitled to some privacy, and she feels that her father doesn't need to snoop around in children's minds. After *Henry Huggins* was published, which was before the twins were born, I thought, *For heaven's sake, what do I know about boys?* So I got a psychology book and read up on the subject and was happy to find that Henry was psychologically sound!

Q: Have you had to do research for your books?

> **A:** Not very often. When I wrote *Dear Mr. Henshaw,* I needed some knowledge of the trucking business, so my husband and I went to Salinas, where I talked to some truckers and climbed up in one of their trucks to see what it felt like. Afterward I thought that maybe those men had been pulling my leg, so from then on I would send my husband out. After *Dear Mr. Henshaw* was published, I heard from a number of sons of truck drivers. One said, "How come you know so much about trucks?" I wrote a picture book called *Lucky Chuck* about a boy with a beat-up

motorcycle. There was no way I was going to talk to motorcycle riders, so my husband went to a motorcycle dealership where there were some young men just hanging around. They became interested and said what I needed was a certain booklet, which they gave me. So that's how I learned about motorcycles.

Q: You've written with affection about cats, dogs, and mice. Have you had many pets of your own over the years?

A: We don't have one now, but we did have the cat I mentioned before, the one that came with the house we bought in Berkeley. It was a very intelligent animal and a great joy to have around, although as I wrote in *My Own Two Feet*, it ruled us with its iron paw in a furry glove. Our bedroom was so low that it could jump in through the window. We tried opening the top of the window, but then it would sit on the sill and throw itself against the window to rattle it. Once it jumped in with a robin in its mouth. And once it jumped in pursued by an enemy cat. A fight started right by the bed. Still, it was a lovely cat, and I wrote about that cat in *Socks*.

Q: Do you ever wonder how you survived some of the unfeeling teachers you had when you were young?

A: It was character-building! When my son had a bad time with his fourth-grade teacher, the principal offered to put him in another class. I felt, no, that he has to learn to survive these things. Everybody has a bad teacher sometime in school. She wasn't really bad. She just didn't understand little boys.

Q: Why did you write *Dear Mr. Henshaw*?

A: It came about because a couple of boys, maybe more than a couple, asked at about the same time why I didn't write about somebody whose parents had been divorced. There had not been any divorces in my family that I had any contact with, so I thought it would be interesting to tackle the subject.

For many years I felt that it was my obligation to respond to any letter I received from a schoolchild. But finally it reached the point where I couldn't do any writing myself if I continued to handle mail. In fact, when I wrote *Dear Mr. Henshaw*, I was partly inspired by these letters, and I made it quite clear that Mr. Henshaw was not entirely pleased to receive lists of questions. You know, only two teachers have noticed that. So my little private crusade went awry.

Q: Would you offer the same advice to young writers that Mr. Henshaw offers to Leigh Botts?

A: I don't offer much advice. I usually say, "Read a variety of books. Write and don't worry about getting published until you're grown up." I think there's too much pressure on children—or they pressure themselves—to feel that if they write, it must be published.

I once received an unusual letter from a class that had a child-size stuffed doll that the children shipped in a plastic container the size of a garbage can to different well-known people. The doll was supposed to spend a day with the recipient, who was to return it with a letter describing the day. The object of the project was to teach the children that they could achieve their goals.

Well, I was so overwhelmed with work and family at that point, there was no way I was going to invite a large doll in a garbage can into my house. I wrote saying I was sorry I couldn't

> P. S. When I asked you what the title of your next book was going to be, you said, Who knows? Did you mean that was the title or you don't know what the title will be? And do you really write books because you have read every book in the library and because writing beats mowing the lawn or shoveling snow?
>
> *Dear Mr. Henshaw*

invite the doll—I have forgotten its name—to visit, but I thought there was a lesson to be learned. If the doll couldn't visit me, it could change its direction and choose somebody else. I hope this was not a negative message. Anyway, I received a very nice letter in response.

Telling children they can be anything they want to be seems to me dubious philosophy, and anyone who tells children this did not live through the Great Depression, when many people were forced to compromise with life in order to survive. Many goals require more education than young people can afford. Talent, family obligations, and the time in which one lives all enter into it. "If at first you don't succeed, try, try again," was a saying I heard over and over when I was growing up. Perhaps that is a message I unconsciously give children. I really don't know. I am more concerned with writing stories they will enjoy reading. The pleasure of reading is the real message I want to leave with children.

Q: What is the best part of being a writer?

A: The best part is being able to create from my own experience and imagination. In high school we were assigned such subjects as "Could Beowulf Make the Team?" and in college every statement had to be documented with footnotes explaining the source. I always wanted to write on my papers, and probably should have, "I thought this up by myself."

A BEVERLY CLEARY READER

The autobiographies:

A Girl from Yamhill: A Memoir (Morrow, 1988)

My Own Two Feet: A Memoir (Morrow, 1995)

Ellen Tebbits, illustrated by Louis Darling (Morrow, 1951)

The Henry books:

Henry Huggins, illustrated by Louis Darling (Morrow, 1950)

Henry and Beezus, illustrated by Louis Darling (Morrow, 1952)

Henry and Ribsy, illustrated by Louis Darling (Morrow, 1954)

Henry and the Paper Route, illustrated by Louis Darling (Morrow, 1957)

Henry and the Clubhouse, illustrated by Louis Darling (Morrow, 1962)

Ribsy, illustrated by Louis Darling (Morrow, 1964)

The Leigh Botts books:

    Dear Mr. Henshaw, illustrated by Paul O. Zelinsky
        (Morrow, 1983)

    Strider, illustrated by Paul O. Zelinsky (Morrow, 1991)

The Ralph S. Mouse books:

    The Mouse and the Motorcycle, illustrated by Louis
        Darling (Morrow, 1965)

    Runaway Ralph, illustrated by Louis Darling (Morrow, 1970)

    Ralph S. Mouse, illustrated by Paul O. Zelinsky
        (Morrow, 1982)

The Ramona books:

    Beezus and Ramona, illustrated by Louis Darling
        (Morrow, 1955)

    Ramona the Pest, illustrated by Louis Darling
        (Morrow, 1968)

    Ramona the Brave, illustrated by Alan Tiegreen
        (Morrow, 1975)

    Ramona and Her Father, illustrated by Alan Tiegreen
        (Morrow, 1977)

    Ramona and Her Mother, illustrated by Alan Tiegreen
        (Morrow, 1979)

    Ramona Quimby, Age 8, illustrated by Alan Tiegreen
        (Morrow, 1981)

    Ramona Forever, illustrated by Alan Tiegreen
        (Morrow, 1984)

SHARON CREECH

Born 1945, South Euclid, Ohio

Sharon Creech grew up in a large Midwestern household of energetic talkers and storytellers. The title of one of her first books, *Absolutely Normal Chaos*, describes well the crowded life of those first years. When privacy was in short supply, young Sharon would head outdoors, climb a tree, and daydream with swelling pride about a secret her cousins had confided to her: that she and her family were part Native American. She thrilled at the thought (whether or not it was true), devoured books on Native American lore and mythology, and went for walks in the nearby woods, where she imagined herself to be the heroine of ancient stories.

From early on, reading for Creech went hand in hand with writing—stories, poems, and plays for her own enjoyment. But the idea to become a writer came to her only years later, while Creech was living in England and leading the life she had until then always imagined for herself as a teacher, wife, and mother.

What prompted her to change direction? The death of one of the great talkers in her life. Suddenly, she recalls, it seemed up to her to fill the silence left behind by her father's passing. Not everyone, Creech realizes, would have had that same thought. But then so much of what is funny and touching in her books has to do with the sometimes extreme and often unpredictable differences in people's reactions to experience. Some time later, while in the midst of writing *Walk Two Moons*, she began to sense her father's presence in the clouds she liked to watch on her walks and in a certain favorite stand of trees. It was a strange, mysterious feeling, and one day she decided to ask her matter-of-fact youngest brother about it. Did he, the poet and novelist wanted to know, ever have the same feeling? Even once? Even a little bit?

"My brother glanced at the clouds and the trees. He thought for a moment. Then he replied. 'Nope,' he said. 'Can't say that I have.'"

Leonard S. Marcus: What kind of child were you?

Sharon Creech: I was an energetic, curious, independent tomboy, one of five noisy children in our family. In the neighborhood, we were known as "those wild Creech kids." At school, I was sensitive (in elementary school, I cried easily). I probably resembled a combination of my characters Zinny Taylor (from *Chasing Redbird*), Mary Lou Finney (from *Absolutely Normal Chaos*), Salamanca (from *Walk Two Moons*), and Annie (from *Heartbeat*).

Q: What is the first time that you can recall wanting to make someone laugh?

A: When I was about eight years old and my parents were shouting at each other, I put on an outrageous outfit (my father's shoes, mother's dress, a wig) in an effort to make them stop arguing. Somehow I understood that humor might work. It did.

Sharon, age five, with her four-year-old brother, Dennis

Q: Who were the storytellers in your family?

A: My father's southern Ohio/Kentucky family was full of storytellers. They could take a two-minute incident in the grocery store and turn it into an hour's yarn. My father was one of ten children, and each of his siblings would try to outdo the others in their tales. My cousins used to frighten the pants off of us with their tales of bears and convicts and ghosts in the woods.

Q: Did you, like Annie in *Heartbeat*, once jump from a swing wondering, "What are we doing here on earth?"

A: Yes, I did. I wanted to have a *purpose*. There is a swing in our yard now, and when I swing on it, I sometimes ponder this same question, although I feel much more purposeful now.

Q: Have you, like Annie, ever had a dream with footnotes?

A: No, I haven't had a dream with footnotes, but when I worked for a short time as a proofreader (two people reading aloud to each other, including the punctuation marks), at night in my dreams, I'd be reading books or letters and reading the

> Mr. Cheevey stood up. "Mary Lou Finney," he said, and put out his hand, and I quickly wiped off the oyster juice on my purple napkin and put my hand out and he gently crushed all my fingers in his enormous hand.
>
> *Absolutely Normal Chaos*

punctuation, as in "Capital *D* Dear capital *D* Dad comma new line capital *H* How are you question mark." It drove me bonkers for the longest time.

Q: Were you a good student?

A: Yes, I was. I loved all the "stuff" at school: pencils, paper, pens, books, and I was eager to learn. I also very much wanted to please.

Q: What did you read as a child?

A: We were not close to a library, and books were not a common item in our house, but I read whatever was around. My parents owned a set of the Great Books, and one day when I was about nine, I pulled one out, intending to read Sophocles or Plato. When I opened the book, a millipede jumped out of the binding and ran across my leg. I didn't go anywhere near those books again for a long, long time. I read *Reader's Digest* and comic books. Later, someone gave us a dozen Nancy Drew books, so I read those, too. In school, we only read from anthologies, and it wasn't until I was in college and graduate school that I found—and inhaled—truly *good* books, *whole* books. I'm not entirely sure, though, that I'd have read better books when I was young, had they been available, because most of the time I was outside: riding a bike, playing Spud or baseball, climbing trees.

Q: Do you recall the first time you went to the theater?

A: In the seventh grade, our class went to a production of *South Pacific*, but I am sorry to say that I had just discovered the appeal of boys and was far more interested in what the boys nearest me were doing. What they were doing was flirting with my friends but not with me.

Q: Did you, like Mary Lou and her classmates, keep a journal?

A: I tried keeping a diary at various times. It was a useless effort, because I'd make three or four entries and give up. I couldn't figure out to whom I was writing. Why would I write to *myself*?

Q: Were you as a child able to see yourself in the great stories of Greek mythology?

A: When we read Greek myths at school, I was annoyed at the reckless behavior of the gods, but I loved the myths that explained natural phenomena, such as why there is winter or why there are evils in the world. In fifth or sixth grade, we must have done a unit on American Indian legends, because I spent a couple of years deeply engrossed in those, much to the annoyance of my family, who had to put up with my new identity. According to family legend, one of our ancestors was Native American, and I fully believed I had inherited all of those genes and had a direct line of communication with my Native ancestors. I did not care to investigate the particular ancestry, but rather I adopted bits and pieces of every bit of Native American lore I discovered. A few years later, I became enchanted with the Italian side of my family and began speaking Italian, as my grandmother did. Unfortunately, many of her phrases were curses. I unintentionally insulted our elderly Italian neighbors and was scolded by them: "Never say that! Only mad big people can say that!"

Q: When did you first realize you wanted to write? When did you first think of yourself as a writer?

> A: From the time I was about eight years old, indoor rainy play included either playing reporter or writing and acting in plays. The reporting got me in trouble, because I made up stories about neighbors and circulated handwritten newspapers. I also wrote funny (and lame) poems for my family, but "being a writer" was not something I dreamed of. I wanted to be a teacher, an actress, a singer, a dancer, an ice skater, a painter. Not just one of those, but *all* of those. In college, I took my first writing course and met a "real" author, British writer John Hale. I was mesmerized by the process of writing, by the way that words seemed to appear magically on the page—where did they come from?—and I was encouraged by my professors. I didn't think of myself as a writer, though, until my first book, a novel for adults called *The Recital*, was accepted for publication in England in 1989–90.

Q: What did living abroad teach you about yourself? Did you find, for instance, that as an American your sense of humor was different from that of the people around you?

> A: I learned so much from living in England and Switzerland for those nineteen years and from teaching international students, and what I learned was less about myself than about other people and languages. I loved hearing foreign languages, so novel and enchanting to my ear. I learned great respect for other cultures. I could see how aspects of my English, Scottish, and Italian ancestors—gestures, inflections, phrasings, even the appeal of certain landscapes—were evident in my own American family and in me. And while, yes, British—and

1 September 2005

Joanna Cotler
HarperCollins Children's Books
1350 Avenue of the Americas
New York, NY 10019

Dear Joanna,

Enclosed, as we discussed, is the manuscript for THE CASTLE CORONA.

What is it? You know I always have trouble answering this question, but I'd say it's a story of peasants and royals and the intersection of their worlds. Like all of my books, there's some of that 'let's walk a mile in these people's shoes and see how they think and feel,' and I hear echoes of *Ruby Holler* in it, too. It's not meant to be a heavy thing, but rather a lighter story, a comfortable entertainment, I suppose.

What is it about? That's the other question I always have trouble answering. I think I'm poking at--again, *lightly*: the sometimes-foolishness of those in power and their ignorance of the 'real' world; and the natural inclination to see others' lives as 'better' or 'easier.' Another familiar motif you will find is the element of story and its ability to entertain or comfort or enlighten us.

So, that's what *I* think. I will be eager to hear what *you* think. As I said on the phone, I know it could go in other directions--it could be more this or more that--but as it stands now, I like that it feels complete (to *me)*, and there is something in that I'm probably reluctant to tamper with too much. But you know I'll *listen* to whatever you want to say!

With thanks in advance for every little and large thing,

Sharon Creech   *Enclosure*

Cover letter for the manuscript for *The Castle Corona*

Chapter Ten: The Hermit

As the hermit gestured toward a straw mat, the King took his usual place, settling himself cross-legged on the floor. Once the King was seated, the hermit silently sat across from the King on a similar straw mat. Neither had yet spoken, for this was the way of the hermitage: silence first.

It seemed to the King that the hermitage was a basin of calm and quiet, and he welcomed this. He doubted if the hermit ever spoke except when the King was present, so what noise would these walls hear? Only the daily shuffling of an old man?

It had been the King's desire to acquire the hermit, and although the King knew that others referred to this as his 'folly,' he did not mind. A King should be allowed his follies. But the King himself did not consider the presence of the hermit a folly.

His interest in his own personal hermit had first arisen when Count

· ·

Manuscript page from *The Castle Corona*. (Note the date: Sharon Creech, a tireless reviser, held on to the manuscript for a few days after typing her cover letter.)

Sharon Creech, dockside, "fishing in the air"

Italian and Japanese and Swiss—humor was different from
my own (some being more wry or more subtle or pun-based,
for instance), it was beautiful to understand that humor—the
need for it and the impulse to use it—is universal.

Q: Did humor play a part in your work as a teacher?

A: Most definitely! One reason I became a teacher was because
my learning-disabled son had had far too many dour teachers, and he was often, therefore, miserable in school. I was
determined that the classroom would be a place of appeal and
excitement, that not one minute of a student's time would

be wasted, and that the atmosphere would be congenial and warm—and generously doused with laughter. I was full of passion for story, full of respect for each student, and quick to laugh, especially at my own mistakes—and I made plenty of mistakes, especially in the early years.

Q: Are there passages in your books that make you laugh just to think of them?

A: It's a little embarrassing to admit, but yes, and here are some: when Jack, in *Love That Dog*, reacts to the poetry of Robert Frost and of William Carlos Williams; the "socks in the pee pot" episode in *Absolutely Normal Chaos*; the "snakes in the engine" scene in *Walk Two Moons*; and Florida, in *Ruby Holler*, saying "putrid" all the time.

Q: Why do you think you are so often drawn to writing about thirteen-year-olds?

A: That age seems to represent an important cusp: no longer a child, but often childlike; not yet an adult, but often astute and mature. At that age, everything is still possible—"What will I be? What will I do? Who am I?"

When I was twelve and thirteen, the ground shifted and the world realigned in four unexpected ways. We took a trip to Idaho (much like Salamanca in *Walk Two Moons*), and I was in awe of our vast country, of its beauty and its suggestion of limitless possibilities. My youngest brother was born, and I was in awe of him, too (much as Annie is in *Heartbeat*): what a *miracle* a baby is! I went from a small, comfortable elementary school to a large middle school, and I was disturbed by this new world of cliques (much as Mary Lou is in *Absolutely Normal Chaos*).

And finally, my father had a severe heart attack, and I was terrified and unmoored (much as Leo is in *Replay*).

Q: **What do you think of Mark Twain's remark, "The secret source of Humor . . . is not joy but sorrow"?**

A: Hmm. I wonder whether he was referring to the writer (writing humor) or the reader (who perceives it)? I do think humor is stronger or more potent when it is juxtaposed with sorrow. I'm not a fan of jokesters or one-liners or farce. Instead, I am drawn to humor that arises out of sorrow or fear, or exists alongside them. It is also a useful technique to employ comic relief after serious passages, and using humor contrapuntally with seriousness arises naturally out of who I am. I worry a lot, but it is instinctive to counter the worry with humor. It is the primary way I cope with the chaos around me: to look at the absurdity in the wretchedness and slant it slightly, to puncture the absurd through humor. Otherwise, I feel as if I'd dissolve into the abyss of worry and fear.

Q: **Do you have a work routine?**

A: Yes, I suppose you'd call it a routine of sorts. A writing day (as opposed to a travel-to-give-a-speech day or a get-the-car-fixed day) goes something like this: slither into my home office by eight o'clock a.m. and watch the squirrels outside my window; attend to urgent e-mails; review the previous day's work; dive into the next chapter; write until noon (hopefully completing five pages); eat lunch, take a walk, take a nap; review the morning's pages and write a few more; do the laundry; edit the pages done thus far; make and eat dinner, iron, and watch the news; answer mail. In between all that, the phone rings like crazy, and

> Robert Frost doesn't seem to have a very big vocabulary. I bet he didn't do very well in English. But once you get used to his poems, they're okay.
>
> *Absolutely Normal Chaos*

sometimes I answer it and sometimes I don't. I answer it when it's my editor, Joanna Cotler, or my five-year-old granddaughter, Pearl. Pearl says things like, "Nonna! Last night, I woke up and my bed was all cuckoo," and "Nonna! I am a pteranodon today. I can fly and I eat fish. What are you today?"

Q: Do you know at the start how a book will end? If not, is not knowing an example from your creative life of what you have called "absolutely normal chaos"?

A: I know very little when I begin, and I certainly do not know the ending. An image of a person and a place, along with a voice, appears somewhat mysteriously. The image and voice are intense and compelling, and I rush to begin recording the voice, to see what story is tugging at me. I don't peer into the "normal chaos" beyond—that would ruin the fun and the challenge—instead, I dive in, eager to find out what is going to happen and who is this person talking and what story will I find. I only begin wondering about the chaos beyond when twenty or thirty pages are done. Often I set the story aside then and turn to other things (mail, errands, "real life") for a few days or a week while the beginning simmers in my head. With luck, I can then see the overall arc of the book: if it's a journey, I can guess where it might end, for example, but sometimes I have to write much more until I see that arc.

Q: In *Replay*, daydreaming is a form of revision. How important is daydreaming to you as a person, and revision to you as a writer?

A: Both daydreaming and revision are essential to me. Grace Paley once referred to this daydreaming time as "sitting-like-a-dope-in-your-chair time," something she found essential to her work, and I agree. Daydreaming allows enigmatic pieces to float to the surface; it allows unusual things to align. Probably half of developing a story takes place during my sitting-like-a-dope time, and half arises while I am writing. I love revision: the skeleton is already there, and I have the chance to refine it and sculpt it and add meat to the bones—even rearrange those bones if I choose.

Q: Chaos in real life can be scary. How do you make it funny in your books?

A: Hmm. I just lay out the chaos, and it becomes funny—perhaps the humor arises in the juxtapositions, or the selection of details, or in a character's propensity to exaggerate or to give a deadpan rendition of something. When I was writing *Replay*, I tried to describe to my husband the scene in which Leo replays a conversation with his friend Ruby. They've been wondering what it would be like to have a script for your life. Leo imagines students receiving short scripts (e.g., they discover their lives will be too short) and students flipping to the last pages to discover how they will die. Now, this is a sober thing to contemplate, but as it came out of Leo's head, it seemed so funny to me, and I couldn't describe it to my husband without laughing. When I finished, he gave me a peculiar look and said, "That's *funny*?" And I could not explain *why* it was funny. I think you just have to read it, and when you see what comes before and how Leo tells it, I *think* readers would find it funny. When I was a teacher, I could analyze this sort of thing (e.g., "Types and Uses of Humor in Fiction"), but now that I write full-time, I can no longer do that. Perhaps that part of my brain has atrophied. Perhaps I am losing my brains entirely. You never know.

Q: Have you ever known someone like your character Carl Ray?

A: Carl Ray was inspired by a cousin of mine who came to live with us when I was twelve. He was going to stay a few months. He stayed for thirty *years*. Recently, my youngest brother (who was born after my cousin arrived) said that, growing up, he (my brother) always thought our Carl-Ray-cousin was one of his brothers! Like Mary Lou in *Absolutely Normal Chaos*, I was perplexed by this near-mute cousin who had descended upon our yakkety family, and like Mary Lou, I came to a much better appreciation of him (although it took me longer than it takes Mary Lou).

Q: In *Love That Dog* you show that writing need not be something to fear. Have you known that fear yourself? What do you tell young people who say they want to write?

A: I've never known that fear, but so many of my students have, and I deeply wanted them to conquer that fear. I let them experiment; we used good writing for inspiration; I gave them sitting-like-a-dope time to contemplate their stories or poems. When they saw that they each had something truly unique to offer—that they each saw the world in a very specific way—and when they saw that everything did not have to be graded and everything could always be revised and changed and polished, all those things eliminated that fear. It is hard to give advice to young people who say they want to write when you have but a few words to offer them, but usually what I say is what so many other writers say: read, read, read, for by osmosis you will learn what makes a good story and what type of story most appeals to you; experiment with writing short things; try all forms; allow yourself daydreaming time; and have fun with all of it.

Q: Does writing remind you of cooking, or hiking, or any other activity you care about?

A: Earlier I used the analogy of a skeleton and sculpting, and also cooking (simmering); it is also like painting—beginning with a blank canvas and discovering the painting as you go, balancing colors, using perspective to guide your reader. Painting or composing music (neither of which I can do well) are probably the closest analogies I can offer. I sometimes use the analogy of building a house. You lay a foundation; you erect a frame; you develop sections; you plumb and wire; you paint; you add refinements as you go. So, yes, writing is a lot like that, except I don't follow a blueprint, and I often rip down walls mid-building, and I might put the attic in the basement, or . . .

Q: What would you say is the best part about being a writer?

A: The writing. It is that mysterious process of creating something from nothing: of moving from not-knowing to knowing, of being surprised each day by what seems to come out of the air (but which you know must have come from something inside you), of polishing something until it is the best you can do, and then releasing it, because then it belongs to someone else, someone who might receive it as a gift. That sounds a bit soppy, but that's how I feel.

A SHARON CREECH READER

Absolutely Normal Chaos (HarperCollins, 1990)

Bloomability (Joanna Cotler/HarperCollins, 1998)

The Castle Corona, illustrated by David Diaz (Joanna Cotler/ HarperCollins, 2007)

Chasing Redbird (Joanna Cotler/HarperCollins, 1997)

Granny Torrelli Makes Soup (Joanna Cotler/HarperCollins, 2003)

Hate That Cat (Joanna Cotler/HarperCollins, 2008)

Heartbeat (Joanna Cotler/HarperCollins, 2004)

Love That Dog (Joanna Cotler/HarperCollins, 2001)

Pleasing the Ghost (HarperCollins, 1996)

Replay (Joanna Cotler/HarperCollins, 2005)

Ruby Holler (Joanna Cotler/HarperCollins, 2002)

Walk Two Moons (HarperCollins, 1994)

CHRISTOPHER PAUL CURTIS

Born 1953, Flint, Michigan

If you had been a boy growing up in Flint, Michigan, at almost any time during the last century, chances are more than good that you would have ended up working on the assembly line at the city's massive General Motors auto plant, for decades Flint's main employer. Like many of his schoolmates, Christopher Paul Curtis followed his father into the plant and stayed there for the next thirteen years as part of a team that hung the doors on car bodies. It was boring, repetitive labor, but it paid well, and because Curtis also liked his co-workers, he found it hard to quit the factory in the vague hope of finding a better life elsewhere. With his parents' encouragement, he enrolled in college night courses. He kept a journal and took a shot at a childhood dream— writing fiction—although the stories he wrote in those days were, he now says, just plain bad.

After reading several of his letters, Kay Sookram, his Canadian girlfriend and future wife, told Curtis firmly that he *should* be a writer. He had begun to think so too. Even so, it would be ten years from the day Curtis left the auto factory for good to the day he finally held in hand a copy of his first book, *The Watsons Go to Birmingham—1963.*

Curtis's career took off when an unpublished version of *The Watsons* won first place in a writing contest and he was offered a contract to publish his novel. *The Watsons* went on to win both a Newbery Honor and a Coretta Scott King Honor. Curtis's second novel, *Bud, Not Buddy,* received even greater acclaim, winning both the Newbery Medal and the Coretta Scott King Award.

"Stories," Curtis's editor Wendy Lamb once said, "leak out of Christopher like laughter. . . . I marvel," she added, "at his use of humor," as well as at another side of his work: Curtis's gift for showing "how history affects ordinary people."

Leonard S. Marcus: What kind of child were you?

Christopher Paul Curtis: I was a happy, easygoing child. I laughed a lot. People called me Christopher, Chris, Chrissy P. It was all the same to me.

Q: Kenny's father, in *The Watsons Go to Birmingham*, is a great tease and storyteller. Is he like anyone you grew up with?

A: Both my grandfathers were great storytellers. My mother's father, Lefty Lewis, who was a pitcher in the Negro Baseball Leagues, was a tremendous tease—like I am now. When he was doing it to me, I would think, *Grandpa, what's wrong with you?* Now I've got the same affliction. He got the biggest kick out of telling me that if you put salt on a bird's tail it couldn't fly and you'd be able to catch it. My grandmother got very mad at him over that, because I must have spent, stupidly, an hour in the backyard, throwing bread out to attract some birds and then trying to run up behind them and sprinkle salt on their tails.

My father was a bit of a tease. His father, Herman E. Curtis, had a big band back in the 1930s. I have memories of him being a loud, overpowering, huge presence and laughing all the time. I can remember his cigar. I was ten when he died. I got to know my mother's father a lot better. I wrote about both my grandfathers in *Bud, Not Buddy.*

Q: What is the first time you can remember trying to make someone laugh?

A: When I was seven or eight I heard a joke involving bathroom humor that I thought was so funny that for a while I would tell it to anybody who would listen. I knew better than to try it on my parents. I told it to my sister, and she told me how horrible it was. I kept telling it and telling it, and somehow it never worked. I can remember feeling so frustrated, because to me it was so funny. I remember thinking, *Am I not telling this right? What's wrong with these people?*

Q: Were you a good student?

A: I had a two-tiered career at school. From kindergarten up through eighth grade, I was kind of a whiz kid. I was in academically advanced classes. Then after eighth grade I just didn't care anymore. My grades took a nosedive and never recovered. I remember in tenth grade thinking, *This is the year I'm going to start to do it again.* Then again, in eleventh grade. But it never happened. I lost the drive or the will. It drove my parents crazy, my mother in particular. Nobody at the school seemed to notice.

Up to seventh grade I was in all-black schools. Then in seventh grade, I went to a school that was about fifty-fifty black and white, and from eighth grade I was in a school that was maybe five or ten percent black. One of the really horrible things for black children was that getting good grades was considered "acting white." What a hateful thing to tell someone. So I think that peer pressure did have something to do with what happened to me.

Q: In *Mr. Chickee's Funny Money,* Steven has an unusual relationship with the dictionary. When you were a child did you, like him, think of books as being literally alive?

A: I was not much of a book person then. I read magazines, comic books, *Mad* magazine, but I didn't read many books until I started working in the factory. I do remember that the

Christopher Paul Curtis's seventh-grade school photograph

first time a book really meant something to me was in eighth or ninth grade and I was reading *The Bridges at Toko-Ri.* I was reading along, enjoying the story, which was full of adventure. Then I got to the end, and I suddenly burst into tears, right in class! I thought, *Wow, a book can do this?* That was the first time I realized how powerful a book could be.

Q: After high school, you worked in a Flint, Michigan, auto plant. What was that experience like?

A: I stayed in the factory for thirteen years, and I absolutely hated being there.

Q: Can you remember walking out of the factory for the last time?

A: Oh, yes. It was a big moment for me. I was giddy. But it was also very frightening. There was just one industry in Flint, and you had the feeling that if you left that industry you would fall off the edge of the earth. There were guys who had left, and you'd see them occasionally, and they always looked so unhappy. To get to and from the factory, you had to cross a busy street where every once in a while someone would get hit by a passing car. I remember thinking, *If I get hit on my last day, please let it be going into the factory, not going out,* because I couldn't think of anything worse than to have spent my last eight hours on earth in that factory. I can remember being *really* careful crossing the street that last time.

Q: Did you learn anything as a factory worker that has helped you as a writer?

A: We put the car doors on. We did it over and over again, and after a while all the doors would be the same. A job like that gives you time to think about other things. There were a lot of creative people in the factory, one who did woodworking, another who invented games. I would think about my writing. I kept a kind of journal, in which I would write things like, "I hate my foreman's guts. I wish he would die!" I wasn't writing fiction then. But it was writing. I tell kids that. Writing is writing. You're getting practice.

Six is a bad time . . . 'cause that's when some real scary things start to happen to your body, it's around then that your teeth start coming a-loose in your mouth.

You wake up one morning and it seems like your tongue is the first one to notice that something strange is going on, 'cause as soon as you get up there it is pushing and rubbing up against one of your front teeth and I'll be doggoned if that tooth isn't the littlest bit wiggly. . . .

Unless you're as stupid as a lamppost you've got to wonder what's coming off next, your arm? Your leg? Your neck? Every morning when you wake up it seems a lot of your parts aren't stuck on as good as they used to be.

Bud, Not Buddy

Q: The Watsons joke around—at times just to keep warm. The way you write about it, it's almost a survival tactic for them.

> A: Humor *is* a survival tactic. There was a lot of horseplay in the factory. Sometimes we'd throw things at each other. Humor can also be a way of dealing with tragedy. I feel very fortunate to be able to see the humor in a lot of things.

Q: In *Mr. Chickee's Funny Money*, Steven says, "Never felt better. Never had less."

> A: That was one of my father's favorite sayings. My father had a very interesting life. He was in the army during World War II, took a test to go to medical school, and did extremely well. Somehow they didn't realize he was black until he turned up, and when he did they told him that this special program was not for black people. When he left the army, he became a chiropodist and set up a practice in Flint. Then, when his practice wasn't doing very well, he went to work in the factory, starting out on the line and eventually becoming the first black production foreman at General Motors. Then he moved up and became the head of the education department at Fisher Body.

Steven couldn't help laughing. The boy did too. And just as it happens so many times, that good shared laugh was the sound of a great friendship being born.

Mr. Chickee's Funny Money

Q: Was it your wife who first encouraged you to get serious about writing?

A: Yes, she realized I was very unhappy with what I was doing and worked it out so that I could take a year off and try to write a book. She always had more faith in my writing than I did. I thought it was something fun to do.

Q: Why did you decide to write a book for young people?

A: I never did decide, and to this day I don't think of *The Watsons* as a children's book.

Q: Originally the Watsons were going to go to Florida?

A: Yes, in the first drafts, the Watsons went to Florida, but it was like a dead end. Once they got there, nothing happened. Then one day my son, Steven, brought home the poem "Ballad of Birmingham" by Dudley Randall, which deals with the bombing of the Sixteenth Street Baptist Church there in 1963. Steven read the poem out loud, and I can remember sitting at the kitchen table and saying to my wife, "I know what the deal with the Watsons is now." After that, finishing the book was easy.

Q: Kenny says, more than once, "I don't know why bullies always have such a good sense of humor." Do you know?

A: I've often thought that insanity and humor are very close friends. In the great comedians there's always an element of insanity. They're really troubled people! Bullies are troubled people too. You're not a bully because you want to be a bully. Chances are you've got some real serious problems. As far as the sense-of-humor part of it goes, a bully is often really putting on a show for the other kids who are standing around. There's an air of creativity in the clever way the bully sets his victim up. Oftentimes the onlooking kids will react with laughter. Of course, it's not funny for the victim. I can remember being horrified at things that were being done on the school playground.

Q: Do you have a work routine?

A: When I took the year off work, I had a rare burst of good fortune in that I realized that I now had to look at writing as my job. To me, that meant getting up and going somewhere to work. So I would get up every day and go downtown to the Windsor Public Library. I eventually wound up sitting in the children's section. Even now I go to the university library and write.

I'm not one of the writers who needs quiet. I keep going. I spend maybe four hours at the library every day. While I'm there I may talk with people I know for an hour and a half.

Then there comes a time, when I'm close to being done with a book, that I do need a little solitude. When I reach that point, I take the train to Montreal. It's a twelve-hour ride from Windsor to Montreal. I like the little rocking motion of the train. I don't know anybody on the train, and nobody knows me. I plug my computer in, and I devote a total of twenty-four hours to polishing it up and reading it through. I'll spend a couple of days in Montreal before coming back.

Q: What do you do when you get stuck?

A: I like having more than one book going at the same time, because sometimes you get tired of the characters. I wrote

CHAPTER ONE

 SNAKES AND MA

It was Sunday after church and all my chores were done. I was sitting on the stoop of

our home trying to think what to do. It was that time of day when the birds were getting

ready to be quiet and the toady-frogs were starting to get louder with that chirpity sound

they make most the night. I wondered if it would be worth it to go fishing for a hour

afore it got dark. I got that question answered when Cooter came walking up the road

waving at me.

"Evening, Eli."

"Evening, Cooter."

"What you doing, Eli?"

"I was thinking 'bout getting Old Flapjack and going fishing. You wanna come?"

"Uh-uh. I got something that's more interesting than watching you fish, I got a

mystery."

This might not be so good. I ain't trying to be disrespectful 'bout my best friend, but

there're lots of things that Cooter sees as being mysterious that most folks understand real

easy. I asked him anyway, "What's the mystery?"

"I was cutting through M'deah's truck patch and seen some tracks that I ain't never

seen afore."

"What kind of tracks? Were they big?"

"Uh-uh, they's long and wiggly. I followed 'em but they disappeared in the grass."

She said, "How Mr. Leroy doing, son?"

"He's good, ma'am."

"You stop in and give my regards to Mrs. Holton?"

"Yes, ma'am, she told me to ask 'bout you."

"Mrs. Brown come by, axed if you's gunn go fishing tomorrow."

"Yes, ma'am, right after my stable chores."

"She done some baking too, say she hoping to trade for two of them big perch."

It wasn't Ma that baked, it was Mrs. Brown! This made the baking in the cookie jar a lot more interesting!

"What she bake, Ma?"

Ma reached down and picked up the cookie jar.

She said, "You know how Mrs. Brown is, 'Lijah, always trying something new. She baked some sugar cookies and some other kind of cookie she call /./.\" Ma quit knitting and looked over her spectacles at Pa. "Ooh, Spencer, I must be getting old. I caint for the life of me recall what she said they was, can you?"

Pa held up on his whittling, looked at her and says, "Naw darling, I cain't recall neither."

Ma slapped the arm of her rocker. "Oh yes! Now I 'member, she baked them walnut and sugar cookies and something she say she gunn call rope cookies. You's lucky they's some left. Was all I could do to keep your daddy out of 'em."

She tipped the cookie jar toward Pa and he reached in and pulled out a cookie that had walnuts stuck to the top of it and sugar dusted all over it!

Pa bit on the cookie and said, "Almost as good as your'n, Sarah!" He winked at me.

we both knew the only thing worst than Ma's pies are her cookies.

Manuscript page from *Elijah of Buxton*

Mr. Chickee's Funny Money at the same time that I was writing *The Watsons Go to Birmingham.*

Q: **What else do you tell young people who want to write?**

A: Be patient with yourself. Writing, and particularly writing fiction, takes a long time to come to. You have to have experiences that you can draw from, and that's not going to happen right off the bat. Your imagination can carry you only so far.

Q: **You were ten, Kenny's age, in 1963, the year in which** *The Watsons Go to Birmingham* **is set. Did you have to do much research for the book?**

A: I already knew all about the bombing of the church and a lot about the civil rights movement. I remembered the bombing of the church because I had never seen both my parents cry until then. But I did have to research the part that takes place in Alabama in order to get the flavor of Birmingham at that time. Also, language changes through the decades, and it's jarring when it's not done accurately in a story. So I read a lot of books about the 1960s, watched a lot of sixties movies, and listened to song lyrics. There are lots of ways that you can grab hold of a time and get a more accurate feel for what it was like. For *Bud, Not Buddy,* I did research on life during the 1930s.

Q: **Do you revise your work much?**

A: I write in chapters and may revise a chapter seventy-eight times. That may sound like a lot, but to me it's fun. Somebody said that revising is like working with smaller and smaller screwdrivers. You finally get to the point where you're just fine-tuning things with a tiny little screwdriver.

Q: Do you start a book by making an outline?

A: I start with an idea but not with an outline. I may think the story's going to go in a certain way and then get a real shock when it doesn't. I'll have the setting and the characters, but as the story develops the characters tell me things that I hadn't anticipated.

Q: Did your character the Sarge, in *Bucking the Sarge,* come as a surprise to you?

A: No, I pretty much had her from the word go. The problem with that book was that I couldn't see a realistic way for Luther to beat that woman. When I started, I had thought that maybe I would find a way. But I realized that the Sarge was so strong and together that, even though she was misguided, there was no way this kid was going to outsmart her. Then I thought of the old saying, "He who fights and runs away lives to fight another day," and realized, to my surprise, that the only way for Luther to get out of his situation was to leave.

Q: You gave Luther the trip you had originally planned for the Watsons.

A: Yes, one of my characters finally did end up in Florida.

Q: What do you like best about being a writer?

A: There's very little that I don't like. As I writer, I can create people and destroy people. I can stop time and can make it run backward. I have the opportunity to travel and meet great people, to go to schools and libraries. I can set my own hours and make a good living. I haven't found anything about it that I don't like.

After it was finished and before it was published, I'd sometimes read through *The Watsons Go to Birmingham* and think, *This is good!* Other times, I would read it and think, *Ugh. This really stinks!* So I'm prepared for anything. One of my sayings is "I get through life by having really low expectations." Anything good that happens is a bonus. If it's bad, well, I wasn't expecting anything more, anyway. The fact that I was older when I won the Newbery Medal made a real difference. It wasn't as likely to turn my head. I have a good friend I've got to be careful around, because when I'm with him I laugh so hard I almost choke. One of his sayings is "One day chicken, next day feathers." This is now. Tomorrow may be something different. Don't take yourself too seriously.

A CHRISTOPHER PAUL CURTIS READER

Bucking the Sarge (Wendy Lamb/Random House, 2004)
Bud, Not Buddy (Delacorte, 1999)
Elijah of Buxton (Scholastic, 2007)

The Mr. Chickee books:
 Mr. Chickee's Funny Money (Wendy Lamb/
  Random House, 2005)
 Mr. Chickee's Messy Mission (Wendy Lamb/
  Random House, 2007)

The Watsons Go to Birmingham—1963 (Delacorte, 1995)

ANNE FINE

Born 1947, Leicester, England

A s a child Anne Fine was a nail biter. At seven she was
sure her bedroom, which looked out on a graveyard,
was haunted. A young person with strong feelings
about things, she hated to sew and loved to read. She would
read even while out walking. (She still does.) She disliked the
"great poetry" her teachers foisted upon her but memorized
it anyway. She's now very glad she did.

Fine began writing her first book, *The Summer House Loon*,
while stuck at home during a blizzard with nothing to read.
She was married at the time, had recently given birth, and
was feeling hemmed in by all her new responsibilities. By the
end of that snowbound day, Fine had made a life-changing

discovery: that the act of writing—something she'd enjoyed doing on and off since childhood—had the power to make her feel a bit better. "That first book," she later marveled, "was truly light in spirit. When I look back at the bleak, miserable creature who sat down to write it, I can hardly believe that she was me."

Fine finds humor in unlikely places: the emotional chaos surrounding a divorce, a young loner's shaky life. She's made a specialty of family fight scenes, somehow managing to make them seem hilarious, even though in real life they rarely are for those involved. That, she says slyly, is "the transforming power of fiction for you." The power of fiction and the power of a good laugh.

Leonard S. Marcus: What kind of child were you?

Anne Fine: Not at all as anyone else would have described me. They would have called me bouncy and competent. I thought of myself as deeply anxious.

Q: You were born in 1947, just two years after the end of World War II. Did the aftermath of the war cast a shadow over your childhood?

A: It spread a gray tone over the childhood of everyone my age here in Britain. There was little sympathy about. Our parents had gone through the war and for so long been cold and tired and probably scared. So there wasn't anything soft about our childhood. You were expected to shape up. Whine about aching legs, and someone would be bound to say, "There was a lot worse than aching legs during the war!" The 1950s are referred to in Britain as the "years of austerity." There was something drab and exhausted about those years. That's why the sixties came as more of a shock to the British than to the Americans. It was a fairly dismal childhood, really. There was not much laughter around in my childhood.

Q: You had your granny Bertha, though.

A: Yes, she was full of merriment. We visited her every other week, and I always thought my mother rather resented how happy she was. That generational thing. I never worked out quite what went wrong for my mother, but after a rather restrained and impoverished Catholic childhood she was forced out of school to earn some money as soon as she turned fifteen. Then the war came along to rescue her. She joined the Women's Royal Naval Service and had a grand time till, I suspect, she got pregnant with my older sister, and all the shutters closed down again. My parents married, pretty penniless, and things turned miserable. My father was one of those sent, by a lottery, down into the mines to replace the professional miners called up for military service. Within a year or two, he was invalided out and became a post office engineer. He was a marvel at wiring things and became a skilled electrical engineer. By then I'd been born. Then, three years later, my triplet sisters arrived. I think the exhaustion of that wiped both my parents out. My mother barely smiled for years.

A: She was a tremendous storyteller. She had a halo of ferociously permed hair round her head. Her clothes were garish but smart. She always wore high heels and had lots of friends. She liked her drink, and she would send me to fetch her jug of beer from the pub whenever I stayed. Now, of course, I realize I was putting a crimp on her evenings. Without me, she would have been down there, singing along. She worked as a seamstress, and it was miraculous to watch her mending things. At fourteen, I came home with my first miniskirt. It wasn't short enough, and I was going out that very evening and was in absolute despair until she said, "Nonsense! Give it to me," and hemmed it higher in a flash.

My father would come home from work tired out and hear these marvelously convoluted stories my grandmother would have perfected during the day, all conjured out of one small remark someone had made at the shops. He wouldn't take the slightest interest, because, as he would say, "She exaggerates so horribly." For him, truth was king. My first husband was a philosopher, and truth was bedrock to him, too. Me, I've always gone for fiction. If it makes a better story, then it goes in. And, in a way, people who tell tales can get far closer to the truth.

Q: Did you have favorite books growing up?

A: Like almost every British child of my generation, I learned to read from Enid Blyton. You worked your way up through her series. She was such a good storyteller that you ended up reading as easily as you breathed.

Then there were two authors I came across purely by chance. One was Anthony Buckeridge, who wrote *Jennings Goes*

Anne Fine playing with blocks

to School and *Our Friend Jennings*—a whole series of funny stories about a young boy at boarding school. Then there were Richmal Crompton's Just William books, which colored Terry Pratchett's writing life and I know colored mine. William's about eleven and is a scruffy, middle-class boy who is always stalking around his village along with his friends Henry, Ginger, and Douglas, causing great chaos. He means well, but everything he does goes awry. There's also a ghastly girl called Violet Elizabeth Bott, who is constantly trying to join them, but they don't want her, because she's a girl. And then there's awful Hubert Lane from up the street, who is ridiculously posh. William's father, Mr. Brown, is a long-suffering man who hides behind his paper. Mrs. Brown is exhausted by William, though she tries her very hardest always to think the best of him. There's a sister, called Ethel, who is a twenties "flapper," and a grown-up brother, called Robert. Richmal Crompton's stories about them are just so funny. The vocabulary is extraordinarily wide. And she has the most amazing gift for dialogue. Whenever he's ticked off, William justifies himself with sarcasm, his strongest weapon. He launches into these huge curlicued orations, in which he explains how nothing could have been the way people claimed, and he shouldn't be punished but, rather, getting a medal. The stories are hilariously funny.

Q: Did any of your teachers encourage you to write?

A: When I was nine, Mr. Simpson would come in to school on Monday mornings and write five titles on the board—things like "The Lost Umbrella" or "A Day at the Beach." Then he would say, "Away you go," and we would all sit quietly to write our story. I'm sure everybody else hated it. But for me, as it turned out, it was amazing practice to be left alone to do this every week, learning how many characters you can take on board and still sort out tidily by the end. Afterward, he would criticize: "Well, what happened to that spaceship?" or "I think you must have forgotten that you had a princess on page two."

When I was twelve, I had another excellent, if terrifying, English teacher. Miss Sinton was Scottish and could be so scathing. One day (and I still don't know why I did this) I stuck up my hand to ask a question. "Could *I* be a writer?" She said,

"Oh, *you* could," rather as if it was no great compliment at all. But even so, I remember that moment with great satisfaction. I thought to myself, *Yes!*

Nobody in my family had ever written anything, and neither parent had been to university. These days they would certainly have got there. But back in those days so many bright young people were kicked out to work at fifteen. That's why my parents made such huge financial sacrifices, so that all five of their daughters could have a good education. I will always be profoundly grateful to both of them for that.

Q: Did you write on your own too?

A: A little. When I was around twelve, the M1, Britain's first major motorway, was built to pass within three miles of our home. A friend and I went strolling along its verge, not realizing quite how serious motorways are. Up until then, it had been little more than a country road. Before long we were picked up by a police car and brought home—not unpleasantly, just with a "Might be a good idea not to wander on motorways" sort of warning. I sent a little handwritten piece in to *Reader's Digest* and was convinced they would publish it: "The Day I Walked on the M1." Lord knows what happened to that. But most of my writing was for school. I cannot tell you how hard most of us worked.

Q: Were you a good student?

A: I was very good. I really enjoyed schoolwork. It brought the same sort of satisfaction that I feel now when I get a book to come right. I'm not a quick thinker. I could no more play chess than fly. But I do enjoy getting things right.

"What bags?" Uncle Len said ruefully, afterwards.

For when he reached the dock, he had not even a hat or cloak to shield himself from the blustering wind and the ~~dark~~ sheets of dark sea spray crashing over the ~~sea~~ harbour wall. He ~~ran~~ from sailor to sailor. "A boy! Have you seen a boy?" Uncle Will crouched ~~in the shadow~~ looking out for a creature ~~of the harbour wall, waiting for me~~ ~~wrapped in a box as large as~~ ~~in a cloak~~ ~~stowing and flapping~~ ~~by a box~~ ever through ~~trying to hurry~~ ~~heard~~ his piercing whistle ~~the rising storm~~

"Clarrie!" ~~I heard him calling through the~~

~~cloak hood~~ "Clarrie! I'm here! ~~I pulled~~ ~~just enough to see~~ ~~where Will was~~ ~~I'm here~~ ~~the cobbles to join him~~ carrying box ~~was hidden. Then Humped~~ over? Thrusting ~~I raised him~~ "Now keep this safe," in his arms ~~own hood over your~~ "And keep your face. ~~well hidden~~ ~~in~~ ~~sailors & passengers~~ ~~the~~ I turned to the ~~milling~~ crowds milling in the dark ~~the dock~~ and rain. "Where's Uncle Len!" Will pointed. "There. Begging ~~rose~~ ~~line of~~ ~~sailors~~ ladies ~~for help~~ clinging to the rail if any saw a boy ~~a~~ ship slide on a ship." I set off across the cobbles in a wind that ~~fair~~ ~~blew~~ ~~rode~~ the edges of the cloak and fair blew me away. "Uncle Len! Uncle Len!" I see 82

Manuscript page from *Frozen Billy*

Q: Did you write your first book, *The Summer House Loon*, with young readers in mind?

A: I wrote it with no particular audience in mind. I simply wrote it. In a way I was writing about a slightly idealized childhood that I had not had. It's a romantic little comedy about a crush, really.

A competition came up. I submitted it for that and was the runner-up. At the party for the winners, a woman came up and asked me, "May I act for you?" I honestly thought she was going to put on some sort of little show in front of me. I took a step back and politely said, "Yes, please." I knew so little about publishing then. What she was really asking was if she could be my agent!

Q: You've moved many times in your life. Is starting a new book for you anything like moving into a new house?

A: New beginnings for me have always been in September. For years and years I would start a book in the fall, when the children had gone back to school and there was peace and quiet in the house. I can't work against noise, especially music with words or people talking.

We lived in California for several years. I moaned about missing English weather, and my husband took what I said at face value. "If you want weather, let's move to somewhere in America where there is weather." So we moved to Michigan, where we stayed for two years. But it wasn't the right *sort* of weather. That's when I wrote *Round Behind the Ice-House,* which is steeped in a sort of homesickness for the climate I missed so badly and isn't funny at all.

Q: What gave you the idea for *Alias Madame Doubtfire*?

A: By then, Kit and I were separated and I was back in Edinburgh. The lovely Georgian streets to the north of the city have rows of houses with communal staircases. Every other door leads to a private house on the ground floor. The ones between lead up to paired flats on each floor above. There are no lifts. I'd often be on the stairs, and began to take an interest in a divorced man in my block. I'd see him each Friday evening, waiting on the stone steps. Our children were the same age, so I knew why he was sitting there getting so depressed and furious when his children failed to show up as agreed, or were dropped off so late that his evening with them was ruined. And so the book is based on the experiences of somebody I got to know quite well.

Often the best plot twists are born of the need to solve some technical problem. In *Alias Madame Doubtfire* you have the farcical scene—which did not make it into the movie—of Daniel doing his naked modeling. I thought of that only when I realized I needed a showdown between my three main characters: Daniel as Daniel and Daniel as Madame Doubtfire, and Daniel's former wife. I'd probably been reading about naked modeling the day before in the papers. As a writer you have

"Have you seen Miss Henson's new car?"

"That was last year. She came on a broomstick this morning."

The Tulip Touch

to have your antennae out to recognize what might be useful. Another example is that, when I start, I'll use any old working name for each of my characters. But I'll be far more aware than usual of names around me. I'll gradually get closer and closer to the names that I want.

Q: In *Up on Cloud Nine* you had a lot of fun making fun of fashion.

A: Well, I'm an old-fashioned feminist about that. I think fashion works purely against women, against their time, their energy, and their pocketbooks. Fashion really infuriates me!

Q: Esme's such a funny character because she's so totally obsessed. To her the whole world revolves around fashion and, of course, around herself. She says, "It's not as if clothes are just something that people put on in the morning!"

A: Ah, "The World of Esme!" Well, I suppose I like to have a go at certain opinions and assumptions. If you take *The Chicken Gave It to Me*, that's a deadly serious book, even though it's a comedy. I'd hope that a child would finish reading it and never buy another non-free-range egg again. And like Stolly in *Up on Cloud Nine*, I don't have much respect for authority simply as such. You'd have to earn any authority you had over me, and I would rather like to inculcate that attitude in children.

Q: There's something wonderful about the sense of freedom that Stolly has, even though it gets him into such trouble.

A: That's what I love about him. He's impervious to social conditioning. He's based on those children I've known who never seem to be looking around to see how they ought to be behaving. They're somehow self-motivated at every single level. I

And when sleep finally came,

(B) Was it because, the letter hidden under my
pillow, That Mother came so vividly to
my mind. And I every dream

But because, singing under her breath,
busying herself as we sat at
our table selling and ... Uncle Len.
I could ... her voice
and the ocean as clearly as if
I stood ... The dream was
real. Oh, Len You know as well as I, So that
"A Man Makes his Own Fortune,"

(A) That night, I lay so restless.
Through the window, the small
clouds scudding the sky
all the I'd seen
I thought of ships straining at the
tide and the long voyage we all
long to make.
And then I heard my own

Manuscript page from *Frozen Billy*

have a daughter like that. When she was four, she looked at something on her plate really closely for the first time. "What's this?" "Duck," I said. "What? *Duck* duck?" (I could see trouble coming.) "Yes, duck duck," I admitted. "You mean, like, on the *pond?*" "Well, not *exactly*," I defended myself, "but, yes, of that ilk." And that was it. She pushed her plate away and was a vegetarian from that day on. She was so funny and clever—and so very vulnerable and sensitive to pain in the world. She had no carapace, no protective shell. Neither does Stolly. I have a particular respect and fondness for children like them, because for them life is a whole lot more difficult. There's a French proverb that says, "Ignorance and lack of curiosity are the two softest pillows on which to rest your head." I think that's absolutely true. A lot of the people you see around you don't care what's going on in the world. My daughter and Stolly do care, and that's harder.

Q: You describe Stolly as a "jester."

A: I do. I mean that other people find him odd and off beam. But let's face it, in Shakespeare the jester is always the one who's given license to say whatever he wishes.

Q: And he pays a price for it. . . .

A: Yes. Again, that price is awareness. The pain of being aware of what is going on around you is often what galvanizes a person to wit and humor.

Q: Are you also especially fond of Simon?

A: I am. A character grows under the pen. I started *Flour Babies* with just a couple of Simon's basic characteristics in mind—

that he was underachieving and shy. I had the image of him from the scene where the nice teacher is trying to draw him out, and he's just standing there, inarticulately pawing the ground.

Q: The word *explosion* turns up in many of your humorous books, and it's certainly funny when in *Flour Babies* all that flour goes flying. What is explosive about humor?

A: Well, a good laugh can often serve as a release from the pressures, say, of being controlled and disciplined and having to sit still all day at school. I suspect the whole business of writing is like that. You write a book to let off steam. I've just finished the darkest book I've ever written, *The Road of Bones,* and after it was done I felt like a piece of chewed string—utterly exhausted. So I wrote a little comedy—*Ivan the Terrible*—and doing so made me feel so much better. Humor is a healing art, both for the reader and the writer.

Q: What do you say to young people who want to write?

A: That the only real practice for being a writer is reading. If you're not a committed reader, you won't have properly absorbed how writing works.

> They all said he had a great future ahead of him, if he could stay alive and learn to tie his laces.
>
> *Up on Cloud Nine*

Anne Fine writing at home in County Durham, England

Q: Do you have a work routine?

A: What did Thomas Mann say? "None but your best and freshest hours." I try to get stuck in as early as I can. In bed with my morning tea works well for pressing ahead with a story. Editing stuff I've already typed up, I can manage at any time of day. One of the disciplines I was taught at school is knowing when I am concentrating properly and when I'm not. I never work unless I'm concentrating. Once my focus starts wandering, I simply slope off somewhere else to read.

Q: How do you know when a book is done?

A: I come at every paragraph I write over and over again, trying to be "a fresh reader." When I have been through it a frillion times, plugging each hole and trying to iron out every single wrinkle, I reckon it's the best that I can do and then I hang up my hat.

Q: Do you think of yourself as a funny person?

A: Actually, I'm not. But I have always loved the company of people who are, and since I'm a bit of a gannet [greedy person], that works well.

Q: What is the best part about being a writer?

A: The silence. Definitely the silence.

AN ANNE FINE READER

Alias Madame Doubtfire (Joy Street/Little, Brown, 1988)

Flour Babies (Little, Brown, 1994)

Frozen Billy, illustrated by Georgina McBain (Farrar, Straus and Giroux, 2006)

The Granny Project (Farrar, Straus and Giroux, 1983)

Jennifer's Diary, illustrated by Kate Aldous (Farrar, Straus and Giroux, 2007)

The Killer Cat books:

> *The Diary of a Killer Cat,* illustrated by Steve Cox (Farrar, Straus and Giroux, 2006)
>
> *The Return of the Killer Cat,* illustrated by Steve Cox (Farrar, Straus and Giroux, 2007)

My War with Goggle-Eyes (Joy Street/Little, Brown, 1989)

Notso Hotso, illustrated by Tony Ross (Farrar, Straus and Giroux, 2006)

The Road of Bones (Farrar, Straus and Giroux, 2008)

The Summer House Loon (Crowell, 1979)

The Tulip Touch (Little, Brown, 1997)

Up on Cloud Nine (Delacorte, 2002)

DANIEL HANDLER

Born 1970, San Francisco, California

"F ate," Daniel Handler once said, "is like a strange, unpopular restaurant, filled with odd waiters who bring you things you never asked for and don't always like." Handler learned this lesson early and well by listening to his father's harrowing tales of survival during the Holocaust and by absorbing other, happier family stories, like the one about how his parents first met—by chance, as fellow audience members at the opera. Handler himself might not have written A Series of Unfortunate Events had it not been for an editor who, based on a reading of his adult fiction, advised him that he had a talent for writing for ten-year-olds. Handler had not been pleased at this news—not until he realized that some of his favorite childhood books were still among his favorites. Suddenly, it struck him as remarkable that this could be so. He decided to take the editor's suggestion and to write not one children's novel but a series of thirteen. Why so many? Why *not*? As Lemony Snicket would later observe, "Taking one's chances is like taking a bath, because sometimes you end up feeling comfortable and warm, and sometimes there is something terrible lurking around that you cannot see until it is too late and you can do nothing else but scream and cling to a plastic duck."

Leonard S. Marcus: What kind of child were you?

Daniel Handler: I always had lots of friends. I was sort of a court jester. I was never quite in the upper echelons of popularity, but I was funny enough not to be beaten up by the people who were in the upper echelons.

Q: Were you considered a precocious child?

A: I have a distinct memory of being called "precocious" in fourth grade, as an insult, by a teacher. I'd never heard the word, so I went and looked it up. I associated it with the word *precious*, which I knew could mean "dear and valuable" in that sickly sort of way. But I didn't see how *that* could apply to me, and when I finally found *precocious* in the dictionary, I couldn't see how it could be an insult. We were a gifted class of snooty fourth-graders, and the teacher may have been in over her head in a thousand ways.

Q: Apart from that experience, did you like school?

A: Oh, yes. I was reading a lot and thinking a lot and was a very good student.

Q: It sounds like you knew a lot of words.

A: The primary advantage of a large vocabulary when you're young is entirely different from the primary advantage of a large vocabulary when you're an adult. When you're an adult it's so you can describe things with precision, and when you're a child it's mostly so that you can insult people without their knowing it or otherwise baffle them. A child with a large vocabulary is a trusted child. The idea is that a bookworm is not the kind of child who would ever get into any trouble. If, however, you are the kind of bookworm that I was, and you're reading *Confessions of an Opium Eater,* you are probably somewhat likelier to get into trouble than a child who knows fewer words.

I learned at an early age that formality is a very powerful weapon. I went through a very long necktie phase in early high school. In high school I had a job playing cocktail piano. I could play well enough to fake my way through a bunch of show tunes. I would play at private parties and fashion shows. It was a wonderful job for a young man, because it paid well and it was easy. One of the side benefits was that it meant that I owned a tuxedo. I found that I could go anywhere in a tuxedo, unquestioned, as opposed to in regular teenage garb, in which you can scarcely go anywhere. So my friends and I would get all dressed up and go to one of the hotels that had a penthouse restaurant. We would stop at the penultimate floor, get out, and hang out on the fire escape, where there was a huge view

Daniel Handler, age eight or nine (out of uniform and scowling in foreground), at a Cub Scout knot-tying session

of the city. Ordinarily, no one in their right minds would let teenagers through the lobby of a hotel and into an elevator that led to a bar to which they were not allowed to go. But because we were dressed up, it threw them off, and by the time they thought, *Wait a minute*, it was too late.

Q: Was there a lot of laughter in your house growing up?

A: Oh, absolutely. We ate together every night, and the point would be to throw around as many jokes as possible. Not so much jokes like "What did the ostrich say to the rabbi?" We might talk about our day, but always poking fun.

Opera was also big at home, because both my parents were opera fans. They met at the opera when they were each in the audience as other people's dates. I saw a lot of opera as a child, and then I sang in a boys' chorus that was an adjunct to the San Francisco Opera. Whenever they needed urchins, they would call upon us.

Q: What was Halloween like at the Handler household?

A: It was a wondrous time, because everyone from my school came to my neighborhood for candy. My friends and I would roam the streets in packs. I did a lot of rubber masks and amorphous, textile-based drapery. I always thought that if you're sneaking around in the middle of the night you should be something spooky and sinister. To this day I don't understand why some people dress up as exemplars of humanity—as nurses, for instance. After seeing a movie called *Satan's Ball*, which is about a formal masqued ball that takes place in a zeppelin, I remember asking my parents if I could just wear a little black mask, and maybe a suit and top hat. I was sure no one would know who I was. But my parents made the sensible point that in an outfit like that I would probably be recognized.

Q: Tell me about *The Bears' Famous Invasion of Sicily*, which you've said was your favorite childhood book.

A: I was very, very young when I found my mother's copy on the shelf among the hundreds of books at home. It wasn't singled out for me. I just found it, and I found it endlessly fascinating. I still do. It's an action-packed, outlandish book. It slips into verse and into philosophizing, and it has a great cast of characters. At the center of it is a story that's very sad and that doesn't seem to have any clear moral whatsoever about a bear cub being kidnapped by humans, and the bears in the end turning out to be just as bad as the humans. It doesn't teach you anything that you could apply to life—except that it's *shaped* like life, in that there's a mess of things, and you try to do some good, and you try to make good decisions, but it's never as simple as you wish it were.

DANIEL HANDLER 89

A couple of the characters who are listed at the beginning never actually make it into the story. My favorite is the werewolf. The narrator says, "It is possible that he may never appear in our story. In fact, as far as we know he has never appeared anywhere, but one never knows. He might suddenly appear . . . and then how foolish we should look for not having mentioned him." I can imagine finding that on the back cover of a book like *Harriet the Spy:* "There might be a werewolf!" For a narrator who's beginning a story to say that he has no idea what will happen later in the story, when the whole book is in your hands, is just a delicious idea to a child.

Q: Lemony Snicket has some of the same tricks up his sleeve.

A: As a child one of the first Marx Brothers' movies I saw was *The Marx Brothers Go West.* Groucho ties up a thug, binds his mouth, and then turns to the camera and says, "This is the best gag in the picture!" I thought, *Everything about this is marvelous!* I couldn't believe that so much could be happening at once: there was the picture on the screen, and the pun on "gag," and the self-reflective moment that made fun of all the other bad puns throughout the movie. Now I get wonderful letters from children who have found a Snicket moment—it may just be nine words—about which they say, "This is the *best* thing I've ever read."

Q: When did you discover the books of Edward Gorey?

A: The first book I knew by him was *The Blue Aspic.* I was in first or second grade. When I became old enough to have an allowance, it was the first book I bought with my own money. It's about opera and murder, and there was something so believable about it all. It seemed like maybe Edward Gorey was chronicling something that had really happened. This had something to do with the fact that the book was designed to look old. It felt like a glimpse into a world that I knew nothing about—a world that was spooky, and full of mystery, and ridiculous. He has a trilogy called *The Vinegar Works*. It's made up of *The Gashlycrumb Tinies*, which is an alphabet book, and *The Insect God*, which is a long poem about a girl who gets kidnapped by a cult that worships bugs, and then *The West Wing*, which is text-free—just pictures of strange rooms in a house. As a child it never occurred to me that it was nonsense to say the three books were actually somehow linked. I assumed that there *must* be a link. I can remember paging through *The West Wing* struggling to figure out what it could possibly have to do with *The Insect God*. Later I realized that Gorey hadn't been skulking around mansions taking notes and sketching real people, that this was all just something that came out of his head. But at the time it felt so mystical. It felt like the Torah—something that

Perhaps one night, when you were very small, someone tucked you into bed and read you a story called "The Little Engine That Could," and if so then you have my profound sympathies, as it is one of the most tedious stories on Earth. The story probably put you right to sleep, which is the reason it is read to children.

The End

had been passed down that had all this mythology attached to it and that itself was full of myth.

What's so perfect about *The Gashlycrumb Tinies* is that he says, "Isn't it awful that all of these children have been killed in such terrible ways—and now let me list them alphabetically for you to help you learn the alphabet!" It's all the more hilarious because he never says, "Oh, isn't this hilarious?" Books that were pitched as hilarious were never as funny to me as books that had a deadpan feel to them, like Roald Dahl saying, "Isn't it awful that that peach ran over those two wicked aunts?" or, "Thank goodness it ran them over." He never says, "Isn't it funny?" He lets you decide. Books that called themselves "goofy" mortified me when I was a child, and they still mortify me.

Q: Did you ever write Edward Gorey a letter?

A: It would have seemed to me that there would be no way to write to him. You know, you would have to write it in blood and wait for the raven to pick it up. It would never have occurred to me that you could write to him care of some address in the back of a book.

Q: Your father left Germany to escape the Holocaust. Did you hear about his experiences when you were young?

A: Oh, absolutely. There were the surviving members of my family who had gotten out, and then there were those who hadn't made it out. The notion that things could get so bad that you would need to flee made a big impression on me. My father would tell the story over and over of when the Gestapo would come and his mother would have my father and his brother go into the woods behind the house and play so they wouldn't see what happened. There would be this sinister-looking person knocking on the door, and then the children would be forced to go out and play, and then the children would come back and everyone in the house would be upset, but the children would not know why. The scene repeated itself with such frequency that eventually they decided that they had to leave.

I realized that the people who survived and the people who didn't were not divided by virtue. They were divided by accident. It didn't matter how great you were. You still might not have made it. Stories from that time tap into the really good stories, like the one in which at any moment your kindly father might marry a wicked woman and you would find yourself spreading bread crumbs in the forest. Things like that can happen, you realize, not because you're a bad person, but just because they sometimes do happen. My father's side of my family was full of these stories. The Germans on the train were checking everyone's papers, and then somebody tossed something out the window to create a distraction and the Germans lost track of where they had checked and where they hadn't checked and so they skipped a car, and that's why Great Uncle Leo is now living in L.A. Those are the best kinds of stories, not only because, as in that case, they're true, but also because they acknowledge something basic about the world. It makes you go through third grade knowing that the only reason why you are friends with this other boy is because you sat down next to him because your teacher assigned you to that seat, and because it then turned out that you lived near each other and so you walked home together and now he's one of your best friends. It's not because you found each other amongst a thicket of people. It came about through a series of accidents. Even though my childhood was shaped nothing like the Holocaust, I saw accidents everywhere rather than providence.

Q: Why did you take up the accordion? Was it really to drive your parents crazy?

A: I already played the piano. It was my ambition in college to join a band, and it suddenly occurred to me that I could probably play the accordion because it had a keyboard on one end. So I bought one. I'm still not very good at it. It's just that if you play the accordion at all, you're bound to be the best accordion player that anybody around you knows.

Q: When did you decide you wanted to be a writer?

A: I don't remember a time when I wanted to be anything else.

Q: Why did you want to write books for young readers?

A: My editor suggested it after she had read my first novel, *The Basic Eight*, which is set in a high school. *The Basic Eight* isn't a book for young people, but it made my editor, Susan, think that I could write for young people. That's when she sent me an envelope full of children's books, which I thought were dreadful, and then I reread some of my favorite childhood books, and then—even though I told her I couldn't write for children—I began to have this idea.

That's what always happens to me: I have a clear idea for a story right away, and then as I'm writing it I find that it has more twists and corners than I knew. I told Susan there would be three children and they would be orphans and they would go to a new guardian every time and that Count Olaf would pursue them and there would be a library at each stop where they would learn interesting things but that those things would not help them. And then I said there would be thirteen volumes. That was the only thing that worried her, not because there was anything wrong with the idea. It was just that she said no publisher in their right mind would offer an unknown author a contract for that many books. At that point, I had written the first chapter of *The Bad Beginning,* and I had tiny two-paragraph summaries of the rest of that book and of *The Reptile Room* and *The Wide Window.* They signed me up for four. I said to my agent, "We're talking about four books, even though I only gave them the idea for three?" She said, "Don't worry, Daniel, they're *never* going to publish four."

Q: Was it hard finding the right tone for the books?

A: No, because it is a tone that is dear to my heart: dire and ridiculous and prone to unreliable philosophical digression. I think it's basically the way I talk.

The silliest books in the series tend also to be the darkest. It's almost as if one needs to make broader jokes to balance out a more dire situation. For instance, there's a lot of slapstick in *The Penultimate Peril,* and there's also the death of a character to whom we've become quite attached. That death is not slapsticky at all. It's very tragic and ghastly. It's not that I think, *Oh, there are six really violent parts here, so I'd best put in six really broad jokes.* But I've noticed that that tends to be the case.

Q: You've put the word *penultimate* on the map for a lot of readers.

A: I certainly hope so. It was embarrassing when I would be interviewed for that book by fully grown adults who were of the

opinion that *penultimate* meant "last." There was one headline
to an article that read, "The Penultimate Book from the Penultimate Pen." They really meant "Ultimate," but not even that,
really, except in the World Wide Wrestling Federation sense of,
you know, "Big and Great." By and large, children who read
the book are more likely either to look up the word or to figure
out its meaning, whereas adults are more apt to fake it. That
has been one of the pleasures of meeting my readers: hearing
an eight-year-old explain *ersatz* to an adult who has heard the
word a million times but never gotten a grip on it.

**Q: Even the adult characters who aren't cruel, like Mr. Poe, don't
pay enough attention to the children.**

A: That's the permanent gulf between adulthood and childhood. I see it now as I'm raising a child. What's important to
my son, who is now three and a half, may be deciding which
Matchbox car to take downstairs while he's putting on his
shoes, while I'm looking at the clock and realizing that he has
to put on his shoes right now and that he can't pause over the
Matchbox cars. We're both completely baffled by and impa-
tient about the other one's priorities. There's a point in *The
Reptile Room* where the Baudelaires are afraid to be alone in
the car with Count Olaf. He and Mr. Poe are negotiating over
who's going to be in what car. That was sort of dredged up
from my own childhood, when automobile logistics and car-
pooling were constantly being discussed. How were we going
to get there? Which of course was never of any interest to me. I
would think, *Why do we have to talk about this all over again?* The
point is: I just want to be *here*, and then I want to be *there* later.
So the Baudelaires, in more dire circumstances than I ever was

in, are nevertheless in an identical situation, and the humor lies in some people finding it so important to talk about those things, while others do not.

Q: Did writing so many books feel like running a marathon?

A: First let me say that I would be one of the last people ever to run a marathon. For me it was more like preparing an enormous and elaborate meal, which is a lot of trouble. Sometimes midway through you think, *Why have I agreed to do this?* And the guests are about to arrive, and nothing is near done, and nothing is quite as delicious as you'd hoped.

Q: The last chapter of *The End* is very long. Is that because you didn't want the series to end?

A: I wanted it to end like a Russian novel. I wanted a lengthy ending. I had had this fantasy for a long time that the end would be thousands and thousands of pages long. I even imagined that A Series of Unfortunate Events would eventually be collected in two volumes, and that the first volume would contain books one through twelve, and the second volume would be thirteen.

Q: How did you feel when you did finish it?

A: It was with some sadness that I completed the thirteenth volume, but not really reluctance. I was telling a story and I knew where it was headed, and then I got there. There was really nothing more to it.

Q: Do you see a sense of humor developing in your son?

A: Absolutely. Currently, he loves to sing songs that he already knows and make all the words start with the same letter. "Bou

From: Susan Rich
Sent: Friday, May 5, 2006
To: Daniel Handler
Subject: Unmixed metaphors

Daniel, I noticed a metaphor in The End that might be too similar to one you've already used:

The Slippery Slope:

When you have many questions in your mind, and you suddenly have the opportunity to ask them, the questions tend to crowd together and trip over one another, much like the passengers on a crowded train when it reaches a popular station.

The End:

The Baudelaires felt all of their questions trip over each other in their heads, like frantic passengers deserting a sinking ship.

From: Daniel Handler
Sent: Monday, May 08, 2006
To: Susan Rich
Subject: Re: Unmixed metaphors

Maybe the below?
I'll call you soon.

The Baudelaires felt all of their questions tangle up together in their heads, like a nest of snakes fighting over the same piece of fruit.

D.

E-mail exchange between Daniel Handler and editor Susan Rich during the making of *The End*

From: Susan Rich
Sent: May 8, 2006
To: Daniel Handler
Subject: Re: Re: Unmixed metaphors

I think you could get away with less, . . . [and say]
something like:

The Baudelaires felt all of their questions tangle up
together in their heads, like frantic snakes deserting a
sinking ship.

Or, I dunno:

The Baudelaires felt all of their questions bump into
each other in their heads, like frantic sailors deserting a
sinking ship.

But otherwise, the snakes are good, too.

From: Daniel Handler
Sent: Monday, May 08, 2006
To: Rich, Susan
Subject: Re: Re: Re: Unmixed metaphors

I'll think on this. Can we talk at 10:30 my time or will
you be at lunch?

D.

bar by bunshine, by bonly bunshine . . ." He can only do about a line before he collapses with laughter. Even at a very early age, when my wife and I would put him to sleep and we'd be having dinner, the monitor would come on and we would hear him laughing by himself. Even when he had no words whatsoever, he was already finding the world hilarious.

These days, the way I can make Otto laugh the hardest is with deadpan humor. If he sits on my lap and I say, "OK, one shoe goes on your ear, and the other one goes on your nose"—and I definitely *don't* say, "Isn't that silly?"—he'll think that's hilarious. He and I have this game where we'll be walking outside and he'll say, "Say 'no flowers, no flowers.'" And I'll say, "If I see a single flower, I'm going to go through the roof!" And then he'll point to a flower. Then he'll scan ahead and say, "Say 'no dump truck.'" And I'll say, "If there's a single dump truck, I'll eat you up!" He loves this game where I'm always about to go mad.

Q: Do you keep to a daily schedule?

A: I write Monday through Friday from nine to three. I like to think that I stop working around the time that everyone else wants to stop working. Most people have to fake it for another couple of hours. Then I usually go for a walk and buy food for dinner and cook it.

Q: So you are a big cook.

A: I am, which is why A Series of Unfortunate Events is so stuffed with food. I think that food is one of the terrors and pleasures of children. A meal full of things that you don't

> Just about everything in this world is easier said than done, with the exception of "systematically assisting Sisyphus's stealthy, cyst-susceptible sister," which is easier done than said.
>
> *The Hostile Hospital*

like, and which you're going to be forced to eat, can be such a nightmare for a child. And then there are those few rare days when you're with someone who says, "Why not? Double scoops for everyone!" And you can't believe your luck, and you remember that day for the rest of your life.

Q: Was much revision work needed?

A: I'll have a first draft that is long and shaggy and a complete mess. Then I gradually hack away at it, taking out what is unnecessary or not working in some other way. You have to write for a certain number of years before you can realize that you can let some of it go. I was always writing as a child. At school, you'd always have to turn in rough drafts and then you had to turn in the final draft, and you'd maybe change a couple of words, but basically you'd just write it over again in neater handwriting. It was so difficult then to write two pages, but the idea that you would write eight pages and then turn it into two pages in second grade—I just can't picture that. When I talk with adults who are studying writing, I find that the idea that you would throw a lot of it away is too much to bear, and it's only as you get more practice at it that you get more comfortable with the idea. While I was writing A Series of Unfortunate Events, I threw away thousands of pages.

Q: What do you do when you don't know what to write next?

A: Sometimes I'll take a walk, but my rule of thumb is to continue writing even when it's not going well, because in the course of two days I might write fifteen terrible pages and then one sentence that points me in the direction that I want to go. I would rather keep writing than wait for the muse to come.

Q: Are you looking forward to the time your son will be ready to read your books?

A: I sort of dread it.

Q: What do you like best about writing for young people?

A: You never love a book the way you love a book when you're ten. I've been lucky enough to end up in that space in many children's heads.

A DANIEL HANDLER READER

The Beatrice Letters (as Lemony Snicket) illustrated by Brett Helquist (HarperCollins, 2006)

Lemony Snicket: The Unauthorized Autobiography (HarperCollins, 2002)

A Series of Unfortunate Events (as Lemony Snicket):

The Bad Beginning, illustrated by Brett Helquist
(HarperCollins, 1999)

The Reptile Room, illustrated by Brett Helquist
(HarperCollins, 1999)

The Wide Window, illustrated by Brett Helquist
(HarperCollins, 2000)

The Miserable Mill, illustrated by Brett Helquist
(HarperCollins, 2000)

The Austere Academy, illustrated by Brett Helquist
(HarperCollins, 2000)

The Ersatz Elevator, illustrated by Brett Helquist
(HarperCollins, 2001)

The Vile Village, illustrated by Brett Helquist (HarperCollins,
2001)

The Hostile Hospital, illustrated by Brett Helquist
(HarperCollins, 2001)

The Carnivorous Carnival, illustrated by Brett Helquist
(HarperCollins, 2002)

The Slippery Slope, illustrated by Brett Helquist
(HarperCollins, 2003)

The Grim Grotto, illustrated by Brett Helquist
(HarperCollins, 2004)

The Penultimate Peril, illustrated by Brett Helquist
(HarperCollins, 2005)

The End, illustrated by Brett Helquist (HarperCollins, 2006)

CARL HIAASEN

Born 1953, Plantation, Florida

C arl Hiaasen has long believed that he has two sets of readers: fellow Floridians, who know life in the Sunshine State as well as he does; and readers from everywhere else, who imagine he has to *invent* the oddball characters and ludicrous events that fill his darkly comic novels. To Hiaasen, the state of Florida is a place both to love and to be appalled by—an oasis of rare natural wonders and a slag heap of goofy, strange, and (mostly) disreputable people. In all his years as a writer, Hiaasen has never run out of two-bit crooks and ne'er-do-wells in need of a good skewering or kick in the pants. He doubts he ever will.

In 1974, after graduating from college with a journalism degree, Hiaasen cut his teeth as a reporter for a small-town Florida newspaper. He then joined the staff of the *Miami Herald*, where he specialized in exposing corruption in the real estate and construction industries. Often the misdeeds he brought to light had to do with damage done to the environment. Hiaasen was making a name for himself as a courageous reporter. In 1985, he was given a regular column at the paper, an assignment that allowed him to sound off publicly about everyone from Mickey Mouse to the president of the United States.

Hiaasen had other fish to fry as well. After he and a fellow *Miami Herald* writer co-authored three adult thrillers, he went solo as a novelist with *Tourist Season* (1986), the first of several books for adult readers that take place in Florida and mix murder with mellow, absurdist humor. Hiaasen was a well-known mystery writer when, in 2002, he published his first novel for young readers, *Hoot*.

Leonard S. Marcus: What kind of child were you?

      Carl Hiaasen: Because I was a little ahead in reading, I skipped first grade, which meant that I was shorter than my classmates and that socially I was a year *behind*. Girls really aren't interested in dating the smallest, youngest kid in the class. So I was always a little late to the party. And when you're the shortest kid, you end up meeting a lot of bullies. The character of Beatrice in *Hoot* is based on a bully I knew in elementary school—a girl who terrorized me more than any guy I knew.

Q: How did you cope?

A: In elementary school I lived close enough that I could walk or ride my bicycle to school. But starting with seventh grade, they piled us into a bus to take us to the naval air station in Fort Lauderdale, where we went to school for several years in an old barracks while our high school was being built. It was a long bus ride, believe me, especially if someone was hassling you who outweighed you by two to one. We had kids riding that bus who had been held back so many times they were probably nineteen or twenty years old. They had full beards. I wasn't quite stupid enough to take a swing at a kid like that. If they wanted to trip me when I was going down the aisle to my seat, they were absolutely free to do so, as far as I was concerned.

It was during those years that I developed a smart-ass sense of humor to disarm the situation. I found that if I could make them laugh, or say something funny and nonthreatening, making myself the target of my own joke, it could get me out of a jam. So even at that age, I saw the value of making people laugh. They'd move on and pick on someone else—which was my object.

Q: Do you remember learning to read?

A: I learned to read on the newspaper, sounding things out myself when I was about four. I always loved newspapers. At home we got the *Miami Herald* in the morning and the *Fort Lauderdale News* in the afternoon. The afternoon paper would have some baseball scores that the morning paper wouldn't have gotten in yet. I would read the morning paper to my dad at the breakfast table—maybe one story before he went off to work—and in the evening I would read to him again. My mom was an English teacher and was a terrific help to me too. Both my parents were big readers. So, it wasn't as if I was in a cave, trying to do it on my own.

Q: Tell me about the place where you grew up.

A: We lived in a pretty isolated rural section of Broward County, Florida, on the edge of the Everglades. Where there is now an eighteen-lane highway, there was just a dirt road. We didn't even have a convenience store within five miles of my house until I was thirteen or fourteen. We had nothing else to do but get on our bicycles and ride until the pavement stopped—which wasn't that far. Then we would get off our bikes, and hide them in the bushes or trees, and go exploring, or collecting snakes or turtles, or fishing or boating. Kid stuff. Tom Sawyer stuff.

The population has easily quintupled since I was a boy. It was nauseating to see all the development. I hated it then. I hate it now. All I saw was bulldozers coming in and destroying all the places where I roamed, went fishing, camped out with my buddies. It was all being destroyed day by day. My anger over that has fueled not only my adult novels but to some degree the kids' novels as well—the carpetbagger mentality that you come to a place that is relatively poor and undeveloped and buy everything up and tear down all the trees and bury all the creeks. It was just a blight. I wouldn't live there now if you paid me all the money in the world.

Q: When did you start writing?

A: My dad was an attorney, and he would work at home on weekends, typing up briefs. When I was six years old, he got me a brick-red manual typewriter, and I just started typing on it, doing little short stories and poems and a sports newsletter for our neighborhood about our kickball and softball games. Most kids I knew didn't have any typewriter at home. I had that one for years and years. Then when I was a little bit older—maybe twelve or thirteen—my dad bought me a Smith Corona electric typewriter, which at the time was a very big deal. Both typewriters came in handy, because my handwriting was, and still is, spectacularly atrocious!

Q: Why do comedy and crime go together in your books?

A: Ever since I was a kid, I knew that Florida was a funny place. All you had to do was read the headlines. The state has always attracted wild characters and outlaws. It has a colorful crime legacy. And since most criminals are stunningly stupid, the humor flows easily from their thoughts and actions.

Q: It seems odd that Roy in *Hoot* is unsure what his father does for a living.

A: That to me was a south Florida touch. Because of all the criminals, we also have probably the largest concentration per capita of federal drug agents, customs agents, and homeland security people of any state. I've known a fair number of law-enforcement people, including undercover guys, some who do pretty dangerous things for a living, and they don't always share that information with their kids, because they don't want to frighten them.

Q: Did you become known as the "class writer" at school?

A: By default I guess I was. In high school I wrote a newsletter, again typing it myself, and somehow persuaded the principal's office to run it off. It was a seditious little newsletter that was supposed to be the counterpoint to the rah-rah tone of the regular school paper. I was going to write irreverent, wiseass stuff, stuff that made people laugh. I called it *More Trash*. To my astonishment, it became extremely popular.

Again, it was me connecting with the notion that people really like to laugh and that they'll laugh about stuff that's written in a satirical way, with a point or dig. At that time, the war in Vietnam was raging, and you had the ascent of Richard Nixon. Before all that, during the year when I was in the sixth grade, President Kennedy had been assassinated. The innocence was knocked out of me on that day. I began to question everything. Then the body counts began coming in from Vietnam. Government lies were being exposed. The country was in an incredibly turbulent state of mind. For me it was a time to be irreverent about everything, whether it's making fun of the school mascot at the school football game or whatever. By then, the idea of being the outsider writing about it, the idea of poking fun at the establishment, was in my blood. It awakened me to the fact that nothing is as it seems, and that you have to be cautious and you have to be questioning all the time. That's certainly what led me on the path to journalism—that, and the love of writing.

Q: Did you have a teacher who was especially important to you?

A: Oh, gosh, there were several. I had a very dynamic, demanding eighth-grade science teacher who was great. I learned a lot from her about wildlife and the outdoors. I had a terrific English teacher—I think probably in the eleventh grade—who was inspiring. She was tough, too. I was scared to death sitting in her class. Our papers came back festooned with red marks and checks and marginal notes. I probably learned more from her about the language, and the craft of writing, than from anyone up to that point.

Those teachers stand out. But at some point, if you are going to be a writer, your own voice has got to kick in. Teachers can't give you a voice, and they can't give you a reason to write. That's got to come from inside. And you have got to become your own toughest critic: brutal, persistent, never satisfied. That's the only way to get better.

You have to have some sort of fire burning inside. It may be an unhealthy one for you personally, but professionally if it fuels the engine that keeps you productive, you're going to have a much longer career. There are not a lot of blissfully happy serious novelists. And even though my books are supposed to make people laugh, they're serious books. Serious books generally don't come from a happy place.

Q: Were you an only child? In *Hoot*, you write about the "solemn responsibility" that an only child feels toward his parents.

A: No, I grew up with two sisters and a brother, all three younger than me, so our house was full of screaming youngsters. But I had close friends who were only children, and my father was an only child. He lost his mother when he was about five years old, and I think on some level he never recovered from that loss. I know he felt a great responsibility to his father as well as to all his other relatives.

Q: In *Flush*, Noah and Abby's father is an idealist and a crusader. But he also seems pretty loopy and "out to lunch." Was casting him in such comic terms a way of making him seem more humanly believable, less of a "do-gooder"?

A: I know some men who are like their father—bighearted, well-meaning, but also foolish and hot-tempered. What he does in the novel might be funny to the reader, but Noah understands that his dad's mission is a serious, if misguided, one. The guy has passion, which is important in itself.

Q: Growing up, you had a free-spirited loner friend named Clyde who committed suicide when he was seventeen. Was he the inspiration for Mullet Fingers?

A: Yes, in a way, but that character has a little bit of me in him too. I had a much more normal family life. But like Mullet I was always outdoors, running around barefoot. Being on the fringe was Clyde. He lived with his mom and his stepdad, so he wasn't a runaway. The details are not all the same. But the spirit of what made him Clyde is there. Mullet's an outlaw, and when they were doing the movie of *Hoot*, we had to fight and fight to keep him that way. There was pressure from the studio to have him reconcile with his mother and go back to school. I threw myself in front of that train with everything I could, and so did the director. They said, "We can't have him still out there on his own." I said, "Why not? It's the whole point. You're going to lose every kid who goes to the movie if you have him

> Garrett was a D student, but he was popular in school because he goofed around in class and made farting noises whenever a teacher called him out. Garrett was the king of phony farts at Trace Middle. His most famous trick was farting out the first line of the Pledge of Allegiance during homeroom.
>
> *Hoot*

suddenly, blissfully assimilated." He's a survivor. It's inspiring. It's not telling kids to leave home and live in the woods. It's the grown-ups who are a little thick about it.

Q: You've written that you and your friends would pull up some of the developers' survey stakes—just as Roy and Mullet do in *Hoot*.

A: It stalled things, slowed the developers down for a couple of weeks while they brought out the surveyor again. It didn't really do any good. But you didn't know what else to do. The bulldozers were a lot bigger than we were. And we knew nothing about the politics that was making it all possible: a city council that would cheerlead every tree that was chopped down and every ugly condo that got built. We didn't understand the sophisticated level at which corruption operates and flourishes in a place like Florida. We just knew the wilderness was disappearing, and that it was heartbreaking.

@ (CN): THIRTEEN

@tx1: Dad was serious about getting serious.

@tx: The same morning he was released from jail, he went out and
got himself hired by a company called Tropical Rescue. It wasn't
the sort of work that my father could put his heart into, but I
knew why he took the job.

It was the boat.

They let him use a 24-foot outboard with a T-top and twin *twenty-four*
150s—not for fishing, but for towing in tourists who ran out of
gas or rammed their boats aground.

No comma Normally, my father has no patience for these sorts of
bumblers. He calls them "googans" or even worse, depending on
what kind of fix they've gotten themselves into. But Dad needed
the job, so he buttoned his lip and kept his opinions to himself.

Unless it's a life-or-death emergency, the Coast Guard refers
disabled-boat calls to private contractors like Tropical Rescue,
which charge big bucks. They stay busy, too. It's amazing how
many people are too lazy to read a fuel gauge, a compass, or a

144

Manuscript page from *Flush*

Q: Is that why, toward the end of *Flush*, the bad guy almost escapes punishment by paying people off?

A: Sure, that's right out of the newspapers. I didn't have to make that up. I don't think you do young readers any favors by painting them an overly rosy picture. What are we hiding them from? What are we protecting them from? There is no protecting kids. If they have an iPod and a laptop, they're getting it all. A writer's duty is to paint a true picture. Even if it's a novel, the picture ought to be true. It ought not to be misleading.

My novels are not fantasies. They're not superhero novels. They're about ordinary kids who step up to the plate and make a stand. There's nothing wrong with that. The world is doomed if we don't have people doing that. I don't want to preach. I just want to show that this is what it takes to stop bad things from happening.

Q: When did you know you wanted to be a writer?

A: As far back as I can remember. I was pretty lucky to have had that certainty at a ridiculously young age. At some point in seventh or eighth grade, I entertained briefly the idea of being a veterinarian, because I loved animals. But I worked in vets' offices for a few summers, and I realized after a while that there was a lot of science involved in becoming a veterinarian, more science than I felt like learning.

Q: Many young people who want to write think they have to go to New York City. Did you think so too?

A: Never, because I'd figured out pretty early that you can't beat Florida for raw material. It's a freak show. Once I was working for newspapers, there was no shortage of inspiration or of material that could be mined for fiction or nonfiction. This is a place that writers flock to, because there's so much good stuff to write about. It's an incredible collision of cultures. There are the retirees who come down here. Then you have the Caribbean population—the Jamaicans, the Cubans—the tremendous influx of immigrants and refugees. You have the political conflict and, as I mentioned before, an incredible amount of crime and drugs and contraband. It's a hot zone.

Florida has been a haven for outlaws going back well over a hundred years. People who wanted to disappear would come to Florida. Runaway slaves, deserters from the Civil War, the Seminoles, who were pushed farther and farther south. These are real-life characters who only appear "larger than life" to people who aren't familiar with Florida.

Q: Do you have a daily work routine?

A: I write at home, and with two active young kids, that means that noise is a factor. I put on shotgun-style earmuffs when I sit down to write, which is typically about 8:30 a.m. every day, including weekends. I keep writing until I feel myself start to tire. Then I head for the bonefish flats or the golf course.

Q: Is fishing anything like writing for you?

A: Fishing is my antidote for writing. It clears out my brain completely.

Q: Do you ever laugh at your own work as you're writing it?

A: No. My wife says I come out of the office looking like I've been to a funeral. But I know when a passage I'm working on is funny.

Q: Do you revise your work?

A: Constantly, right up until the minute the FedEx guy shows up to get the manuscript. With humor, every beat has to be perfect, and I work like crazy to make that happen.

Q: Do you know from the start how a book will end?

A: I have no idea how my books are going to end until I'm about two-thirds of the way through. My characters are constantly surprising me. That's half the fun.

Q: What do you tell young people who say they want to write?

A: Read, read, and read some more. I have never known a good writer who wasn't a voracious reader as a child.

Q: What do you like best about writing for young people?

A: The hundreds and hundreds of letters I receive from kids, who connect so readily with the characters, and whose letters are incredibly raw and open and insightful. That's the touching thing about kids. They get it right off the bat.

A CARL HIAASEN READER

Flush (Knopf, 2005)
Hoot (Knopf, 2002)
Scat (Knopf, 2009)

NORTON JUSTER

Born 1929, Brooklyn, New York

Norton Juster wrote *The Phantom Tollbooth*, his first and best-known book, on a whim, to entertain himself and to avoid work on a "serious" book he had just been given a lot of money to write. He dove headlong into Milo's story without an outline and with only a vague notion of where the story might lead. "I'd get an idea and run with it," Juster has said of his helter-skelter "method." Then he'd get another idea. And another. "It was like goofing off. . . . It was fun." Rereading *The Phantom Tollbooth* years later was as eye-opening an experience for him as it has been for anyone. "There's a lot in the book," he says, "that I didn't know was there."

The new author had a degree in architecture and for the next forty years spent a great many of his waking hours designing buildings of one kind or another. Juster kept writing too, but only occasionally.

Meanwhile, *The Phantom Tollbooth* won ardent fans all around the world. As its fame grew, interviewers asked the author what message he hoped readers—children especially—might take from it. The message, Juster told one such questioner, is that there is no message. "It's all about looking at things in a new way—a way that's yours alone."

Leonard S. Marcus: What kind of child were you?

Norton Juster: I was a funny, introverted, introspective kind of kid. I lived very much within myself. My brother was four-and-a-half years older than I was, which meant that he was just big enough to knock the crap out of me and that I couldn't get even or even dream about getting even with him until we were too old to fight. He was academically terrific, a marvelous athlete, and very good-looking. I was the *other* kid. In elementary school, teachers would come up to me and say, "Oh, you're Howard's brother. We'll expect a lot from you." That always scared the shit out of me. And I'd feel great resentment over that too. I resented a lot of things, and I was always either bored or disconnected, which was a great trial for my parents.

Norton Juster, about age nine, off to school in Brooklyn, New York

Q: Do you remember your childhood home?

A: We lived in a two-family house in Brooklyn, New York. I shared a room with my brother. We didn't have a lot of space—just enough for two beds and our stuff. As a kid you don't have a sense of your stuff. But I'll tell you something interesting. Starting around when I was eight, I would go away to sleep-away camp all summer long, and when I would come back at the end of August, I would not remember my room at all. I used to come back with the thought that nobody would remember me, either. So I would sit out on the front steps on the first day that I was back home, hoping that someone would say hello because they remembered me. And then I would go into my own room, where I had a big dresser, and open the drawers and rediscover the things that were in them, because I had forgotten what was there. It was the same with the things on the desk. It was all like getting reacquainted with who I was.

Q: Did you have many toys?

A: I had a lot of toys, but the things that I remember best are the books. We didn't have a lot of books in the house. But I had an aunt who every Christmas and birthday would give me Oz books. Those I loved. And I loved a book we had called *Folktales of Many Lands.* But the real treasure for me was the encyclopedia that my mother and father bought for us, *The Book of Knowledge,* which came in twenty volumes in a wooden case. I read those books through at least four or five times, cover to cover. As a result, I had the greatest treasury of disembodied facts in my head, and I would drive my teachers nuts with them.

My parents had a small collection of Yiddish novels in translation by I. J. Singer—Isaac Singer's brother—and others. I probably didn't understand a word I read, but I read them through anyway because I loved the flow of the ornate, elegant language. I loved sounding out the words—chewing them! A lot of what I write—and I write by revising and revising and revising—has to do with pace and rhythm, and it's almost a musicality of the language that I'm trying for. I think that that's what carries kids into and through a book: the way words come out at them. I think this comes from that early, chaotic reading.

I always have loved language. I loved it even in elementary school, when I was being oppressed by the things we had to read: Sir Walter Scott and Dickens and *Giants in the Earth*. To me, reading every one of those books was a trial—even though, as I now realize, there was a richness to them and a denseness you could almost chew on.

Q: In *The Phantom Tollbooth*, you say that sounds can mean more than words.

A: I've always known that. As a kid I would say a word and repeat it and repeat it and repeat it until it had no meaning and was just a series of sounds. It seemed magical to me—although I didn't think of it in those terms—that I could literally split off the word from its meaning, leaving me with the word as something just to enjoy. That is how many people read poetry—and write it, I think.

Q: Did math interest you?

A: Well, on and off. When I was much younger, I had great difficulty with arithmetic. Somehow I couldn't get numbers into my head. Then I began to do the numbers by color. I know to this day that "four is blue; two, yellow, etc." It would help me to think. As I got older, I got better at math—and realized that math can actually be pretty funny. Any discipline that has the concept of negative numbering has got to be funny. In *The Phantom Tollbooth*, I have the bits about Infinity and Averages—

those are examples of my way of taking mathematical concepts to a ridiculous extreme. I put all of the math that I know into *The Dot and the Line,* which isn't a lot!

Q: Did members of your family have a good sense of humor?

A: My father, who was an architect, was a very quiet, understated man, but he loved wordplay. He was a punster. He'd have a very serious look on his face and suddenly say, "Aha! I see you've come early, since lately you used to be behind, but now you're first at last." I'd look at him and not know what the hell he was saying. Or he'd put his arm around me and say, "You're a good kid, and I'd like to see you get ahead. You need one!" Or out of the blue he'd come up to me and say, "If I give you a cow, will you give me a bag of beans?" I'd think for a second and then of course remember, *Oh yes, "Jack and the Beanstalk."* It was that marvelous sense of things being out of context, of suddenly slipping something into a conversation out of nowhere. It was pure delight.

When you're very young, your natural response to puns is to groan, because you don't quite get what they're all about. But after a while you realize that puns and wordplay are fun. I've watched it with my granddaughter. Now that she is ten, she is beginning to give them back. She's not getting it completely right yet, but it's dawning. At her age, humor is still just a feeling, a vague sense that there are things in the world that are so incongruous and wacky that it's funny and wonderful just to notice them. She will tell me the most pointless jokes, but with such delight that you cannot *not* respond to the feeling behind them. It's a feeling that she will carry with her always—I hope.

Q: Did your father influence your writing?

A: Well, *everything* influences your writing in a way. But, yes, my father was an influence. The other major one was the Marx Brothers' movies, which I loved because they're pure insanity. Nothing makes any sense in them. Yet they do make a *kind* of sense. There's one marvelous scene in which Chico is going over a contract with Groucho, and they're reviewing all the clauses, and finally Groucho says, "That's what you call a sanity clause." And Chico says, "There ain't no Sanity Clause!" As a kid I howled at that, and I still do.

Q: What about your mother?

A: She was the rock of the family. She was in charge of everything, in part because my father was away so much because of his work. She was a great comforter. And she could make anything with her hands, for instance costumes for my school plays, artificial flowers, hats, handbags, sweaters, afghans, crocheted antimacassars. She was also fiercely supportive. When I wrote *The Phantom Tollbooth*, my mother typed the manuscript for me—revision after revision after revision. After it was published, she terrorized bookstores. "What?" she'd scold the clerk. "You don't have my son's book?"

Q: Did you enjoy acting as a child?

A: Oh, yes. I grew up on make-believe, and I loved performing. I started acting at camp, where I did a personality flip and became more extroverted generally, which I realized was more natural to me. One summer at camp, I starred in a play called *My Client Curley* by Norman Corwin, playing the part of the kid with a dancing caterpillar that will only dance to one

①

"Couldn't eat another thing", puffed the duke clutching his stomach.

"Oh my, oh dear, oh my", agreed the minister who was breathing with great difficulty.

"M-m-m-m-f-f-f-m", mumbled the earl desperately trying to swallow another mouthful.

"Full up", grunted the count loosening his belt.

"Thoroughly stuffed", sighed the undersecretary reaching for the last cake.

As everyone finished, a hush settled over the banquet hall once again and all that could be heard were was the creaking of chairs, the pushing of plates, and the licking of spoons ~~thumbs~~ ~~theremin butter per that talk waiters~~ ─ and of course a few words from the Humbug.

"A delightful repast, delicately prepared and elegantly served", he announced to no one in particular. "A feast of rare bouquet ─ my compliments to the chef, yes indeed, my compliments to the chef." ~~He squared, it struck to~~ ~~this quick with a most unhappy look~~ And then turning to Milo with a most unhappy look on his face, "would you pour me a glass of water, please, I seem to have a touch of indigestion."

"Perhaps you've eaten too much too quickly," Milo replied, handing him the glass.

"To be sure, too much too quickly," gasped the

tune: "Yes Sir, That's My Baby." I desperately wanted to be an actor, which of course was a goal that my parents completely rejected. Senior year in high school, I was in charge of the class play, which gave me such power: not only was I excused from class for rehearsals, but I could also choose who else would be excused from class.

Q: Like your father and older brother, you also became an architect.

A: I guess it was in the blood. My early toys were samples of materials and products from my father's office. I guess I just couldn't imagine having a job in which you didn't make something.

I worked for my father for a while. One day I did a drawing and very proudly gave it to him. When he gave it back to me an hour later, it looked like someone had bled to death on it, it was so covered with corrections in red pencil. I was devastated. But I quickly realized he knew what he was doing! He taught me a lot. He designed a lot of schools and religious buildings. He wasn't a very innovative designer, but he was a good craftsman: everything he did worked well. Of course I never realized the importance of that when I was young. I always wanted him to be a modern architect, which he wasn't.

Q: What kind of buildings did you design?

A: When I was a partner in my own firm, we did many different kinds of things. I loved that. We did homes. We did school and university buildings. We worked on several projects at Colonial Williamsburg. We did the Eric Carle Museum of Picture Book Art. We used to joke in the office whenever we got a new kind of project that one day we were going to get a job where we knew what we were doing. There's something wonderful, though, about *not* knowing. Because after you've done the same kind of project ten times, your thinking only plugs in at a certain level. It's when you don't know everything that you have to ask all those dumb questions that are the real questions—and then you venture off into the unknown. Or not.

Q: Everyone knows that books can be funny. But can architecture
   be funny?

A: Sure. In Italy, I once came across a Renaissance-age doorway that was shaped like an enormous yawning mouth, with the eyes and nose up above. That to me is the essence of humor: something you come across that is unexpected. But in the case of a building that you see day in and day out, a joke like that one can get pretty old after a while.

Q: When and how did you begin to write?

A: After college, I studied city planning at the University of Liverpool's School of Architecture. There was a military draft at the time, and I knew that I would have to go into the service when I came back, so I enlisted in the navy. For my second posting, I was shipped to Argentia, Newfoundland, a dreadful place where the Labrador Current and the Gulf Stream meet, generating fantastic amounts of fog and misery. I became a good four-wall handball player, because that's all there was to do there. I also started to write a little bit and to do watercolors.

We were living on a barracks ship, and I began tacking my watercolors up in my room and out in the hallway. After a while the commanding officer called me in and announced that this really wasn't something he wanted to have done on his ship. You know, "Real men don't do watercolors." So I had to stop. But I liked doing it, and I did make a little book called *The Passing of Irving,* which was a story about a mythological being who didn't know he was mythological and wanted to be real. It was not very good, but that's what started me, really.

Q: How did you come to write *The Phantom Tollbooth*?

A: I had always loved children's books. When I came back to New York, I started to work in an architectural office, and I thought, wouldn't it be wonderful to do a book for kids on the subject I was most interested in—cities? So I applied for a grant to write a book for kids about how people see and perceive cities—"urban aesthetics," as I called it in a moment of self-importance. You know the old saying that when God wants to punish you, he grants your wishes? I got the grant, a big chunk of money, and so I quit my job and started doing research. After six months I had accumulated a ton of three-by-five cards and was ready for a break. So I visited some friends at the beach, took long walks, and to clear my mind I started writing what I thought was a short story largely about a little boy I had met a few nights earlier in a neighborhood restaurant. There had been a family with a ten- or eleven-year-old boy in the restaurant, and when the boy had finished his dinner early, his parents had given him permission to leave the table— which really meant, "Go bother somebody else." So he had come over to me in the lounge area, where I was waiting to be seated. Out of nowhere, he said, "What's the biggest number there is?" I already knew that when a kid asks you a question, you answer with another question. Put 'em on the defensive!

So I said, "Tell me what *you* think the biggest number is." He said something like, "A billion skillion katrillion." I replied, "Well, add one to it." Then we started talking back and forth, and we were very quickly talking about infinity—as only two mathematical illiterates could. We had a real fun time doing it. Later, I thought, *There's a cute idea for a story.*

During my vacation I remembered having been the kind of kid who resented very much having to learn all kinds of things at school. I didn't understand why I should have to learn them! I already knew so much from reading the encyclopedia, and I could never connect anything with anything else. So now I had in my mind a character who was a combination of this little kid and me. I began to scribble. When I came back from my vacation, I set aside the book about cities and kept working on the story. I wrote about fifty pages, not knowing where I was going with it.

At that time I was sharing a duplex apartment with Jules Feiffer. I lived on the top floor, and Jules was on the floor below. I pace while I work, and the sound of my pacing—back and forth, back and forth—was really annoying him! So one day he came up to find out what I was doing. I showed him my story, and he took some of it down with him and started to do these glorious illustrations.

Q: What happened next?

A: Jules's girlfriend at the time was working at a publishing house, and she said, "Let me show it to one of the editors." She also said, "Before you bring it in, write up a little description of what happens in the rest of the book." I had no idea what else was going to happen! So I faked something, none of which

Norton Juster with his cat, Louisa, in his Brooklyn studio

actually made it into the book, and I was given a contract. I was scared at first, but then I got going, and I finished the book in another six months and Jules did the illustrations.

Q: You've said that you had fun writing scenes that Jules Feiffer would have trouble drawing.

A: Oh, yes! It started with the fact that when I was a kid I loved books that had maps on the endpapers. So I told Jules, "This book has got to have a map!" Jules has trouble even driving a car, because he has little sense of direction and less affection for the "concrete" world. He lives in a mind world. So when he said he couldn't do what I wanted, I said, "OK, I'll draw the map and then you'll redo it in your own line." That's what we did for the book's endpapers.

From then on it evolved into a game, with me trying to think up things that would give him trouble and him trying to subvert me whenever possible. Near the end of the story, on the way back from the Mountains of Ignorance with the Princesses Rhyme and Reason, and with the demons attacking them, the armies of Wisdom—Digitopolis and Dictionopolis—appear on horseback. Jules came to me when he read that and said that he really didn't like to draw horses. Would I mind if he put the armies on cats? "No," I said, "you've got to have horses." So he drew a silhouette of a horse, and then he drew two more, which were really the same silhouette placed back a little more each time, and then put a soldier on each one of them. And that was as much as he would do.

There's a group called the Triple Demons of Compromise. One's short and fat, one's tall and thin, and the third one is "exactly like the other two." That's one that he never drew! His revenge was his picture, toward the beginning, of the Whether Man, who is a little overweight, bearded, balding guy in a toga. Sound familiar? We had a lot of fun.

Q: It sounds as if writing *The Phantom Tollbooth* was something like *being* Milo: that you often didn't know where you would land next.

A: The more I wrote, the more I remembered about how things had felt to me as a kid. I grew up listening to the radio, adventure series like *Jack Armstrong*, whose uncle Jim became the model for Tock. My parents had one of those monster Stromberg-Carlson radios that stood against the wall in the dining room. I'd be listening to a Western, and they'd suddenly say, "Here come the Injuns!" I would think they were talking about railroad engines. I would constantly be translating, or mistranslating, things I would hear on the radio or that people would say, which I did not quite understand. Unlike today, we had to supply our own images.

Q: You were twelve when the United States entered World War II. Was the beginning of the war the end of Rhyme and Reason for you?

A: No, I wouldn't say that. But I'll tell you something. Rhyme and Reason were not in the book at all in the beginning. As I continued writing, though, I kept having the feeling, and tried to project into the book, the feeling that things could be completely correct but still not be right. That's when the idea for Rhyme and Reason came in. They existed, but they had to be banished—sent away or lost in some way—and then found. That, really, was the glue that held the book together.

Q: Did the war make much of an impression on you?

A: I remember vividly the day it began. That Sunday I had gotten up early and gone over to a friend's house. My parents were still sleeping when I headed out of the house. When I got to Myron's, I found everyone huddled around the radio at the breakfast table. They broke the news to me. Then I ran all the way home and woke up my parents and told the news to them. It's a very vivid and scary memory.

I became very interested in the war, and I kept a map with pins in it for where different battles were taking place. I even invented a board game called Invasion that I played with my friends. I went through a phase of inventing games but never knew how to get someone interested in them commercially.

Q: Did your editor guide you?

A: He was a wonderfully careful and sensitive reader, and he helped me a lot. He was also very sympathetic to my sense of the book. We had one argument, I remember, over the section in the book about Chroma, the character who conducts the dawn. He didn't want it in the book, because he felt it didn't advance the forward movement of the story. I could see what he meant, but I loved the section—the idea of conducting colors rather than sounds, of turning things around, which the whole book tries to do so that you look at things in a different way. We would argue about this, and at the end of the discussion he would say gently, and ominously, "Well, it's your book!"

Q: Milo finds out that conducting colors is not as easy as Chroma makes it look.

A: Well, that's what you learn: nothing done right is easy. In our basement when I was a kid, there was a big workbench with all kinds of tools. In the neighborhood there was an old handyman named Mr. Brinkman. Because he would do a lot of work for people in the area, including for us, my father gave him the run of the cellar and a workbench. Very often he would sleep down there too. He probably didn't say more than a few dozen words in his life. But I would go down and watch him work. He was the kind of craftsman who could put two pieces of wood together so that you wouldn't be able to see where they were joined. He liked me, I think, because he let me watch him. And every once in a while, he would turn and show me something or he would bring me over to the bench and let me hold a tool and direct me about how to hold it. Day after day

I would be absolutely fascinated. He was very different from the people in my family, being so silent, but there was a wonderful warmth to him. I found out that nothing was easy—or should be.

And then one day Mr. Brinkman was gone. My father tried to find him, but nobody ever did find out what had happened to him. He probably got hit by a car. He may not have had any identification on him. I don't know. But I think back, and I realize that that time with Mr. Brinkman, with his sense of craft, was one of the greatest influences on my life. It works for my architecture, and it works for the writing. Not that I'm always totally successful, but in my mind I can't leave something if it doesn't feel right to me. I'll rewrite something endlessly, and it may be just the placement of a comma, or a single word, or the length of a word that means the same thing as another word but has a different rhythm to it.

Q: The Senses Taker, who's such a menacing character, says that if you keep your sense of humor, he can't touch you.

A: Having a sense of humor can be an essential thing in your life. I have a kind of "gallows humor" for times when things are really too terrible. My wife will say that such and such "is nothing to joke about." But I say that it is exactly those things that you can't joke about that you *need* to joke about.

Q: How do you get started on a book?

A: My writing is influenced by my visual training as an architect. When I start writing, I have to see my characters: how they dress, how they move, where they live, who they are. I

> Milo looked around at everyone busily stuffing himself and then back at his own unappetizing plate. It certainly didn't look worth eating, and he was so very hungry.
>
> "Here, try some somersault," suggested the duke. "It improves the flavor."
>
> "Have a rigmarole," offered the count, passing the breadbasket.
>
> "Or a ragamuffin," seconded the minister.
>
> "Perhaps you'd care for a synonym bun," suggested the duke.
>
> "Why not wait for your just desserts?" mumbled the earl indistinctly, his mouth full of food.
>
> *The Phantom Tollbooth*

have to inhabit a world. It's very different for, say, Jules, who doesn't like things, or, as he calls it, "background." When he draws characters, he doesn't like to draw much around them. The other thing I do when I'm starting a story is to write a lot of conversations between characters, ninety percent of which never end up in the book. But it's through these conversations that I get to know them. I have filing cabinets filled with these notes and conversations, all of them written with number 2 yellow pencils. I don't use a computer or even type—just endless scribbled notes.

Q: Are they your magic pencils—things you can't write without?

A: When I was a kid, I used to think there was such a thing. I was always looking for it—the magic pencil I would just have to hold on to, and it would do all the work.

Q: Where did you look?

A: You don't look. You just hope it's going to appear. For a short period of time, I asked my wife, Jeanne, to type up my notes. To make things clear and easy, I put them in a folder and filed them away. But when I took the notes out some months later, they didn't mean a thing to me. I realized why when I looked at some of my handwritten notes, where I wrote big and small and dark and light and with colors and with diagrams and with arrows. With a page like that, I knew exactly what I had meant, because visually I was connected to it.

Q: Do you have a work routine?

A: I'm best in the morning. I have to isolate myself, be quiet, and clear my head. I like putting my mind in neutral and just going. When I lived in New York, I would take long walks with a little notebook and then come back and look over what I'd written. Eighty or ninety percent of it would be junk, but some of it would be good. Later in the morning I would realize, my God, I must have crossed fifty streets, and I have no recollection of crossing them. It was much too dangerous!

At the end of the day, I always leave myself in the middle of a sentence or situation so that when I come back to it the next day, instead of facing a blank page I have something to finish, and I know where to start up again. It's like a running start.

Q: I like that idea. Do you have other ideas or advice for young people who want to write?

A: The most asked question from kids is, "Where do you get your ideas?" Ideas are *there*. They're things you recognize, not miraculous gifts. They're not lightning bolts that come in through a window, and they're not hanging in the air and if you accidentally bump into one you write a great story. Sometimes the best way to make it happen is just to write, perhaps by keeping a journal or diary so that you're always recording things and training yourself to see, or better still, to "recognize."

A character that I will talk about in kids' classes is "the very dirty bird," the one from Context who is always out of Context. One of the bugaboos of our lives is having always to stay in context. Sometimes you only get a fresh view of things if you move away—as the guy did who discovered penicillin, by accident, with the help of a piece of moldy bread. Often important discoveries are made not only by skill but by a sudden recognition of the value of a thing that you may have seen many times before.

Q: What is your favorite thing about being a writer?

A: There are three distinct stages of writing: there's the anticipation of writing, which is wonderful, because you're thinking of all the magnificent things that are going to happen. Then there's writing itself. And then finally there's having written, and being finished. One and three are great. Two can be an agony, because it's a lonely, desolate, insecure time. But the funny thing is that with all the doubt and pain that go with writing, you look back at the writing later and you remember it as a wonderfully happy time. Why? Who knows! But it may be because by writing you've tested yourself and you've fought through. It has meant something to you, so that you can honestly say to yourself, *Wow, it was important for me to have done that.*

A NORTON JUSTER READER

Alberic the Wise, illustrated by Domenico Gnoli
    (Pantheon, 1965)
As: A Surfeit of Similes, illustrated by David
    Small (Morrow, 1989)
*The Dot and the Line: A Romance in Lower
    Mathematics* (Random House, 1963)
Otter Nonsense, illustrated by Eric Carle
    (Philomel, 1982)
The Phantom Tollbooth, illustrated by Jules
    Feiffer (Epstein & Carroll, 1961)

DICK KING-SMITH

Born 1922, March Bitton, Gloucestershire, England

Dick King-Smith was a fifty-six-year-old schoolteacher and grandfather in the year that he first became a published author. He had always been good with words and bad with money, and he had tried earning a living, at one time or another, as a farmer, a salesman, and shoe factory worker. He'd also served his country as a foot soldier during World War II.

Farming was what he'd always dreamed of doing, though in his boyhood fantasy this had meant something not very different from playing with one's pets all day outdoors. But, after the war, when it came to doing the real thing, King-Smith adjusted to the long, hard hours of backbreaking labor and did his level best for his cattle, poultry, pigs, and crops. Even so, the young man who'd studied Greek and Latin in school and liked to scribble silly poems for his own entertainment never managed to turn a penny of profit by working the land. After many years of trying to do so, he decided that teaching young children might be an easier way to make a living.

King-Smith had always had a knack for telling stories. But it was not until his teaching years that he first sat down to write a story for children. He found that he enjoyed imagining what a pig and a dog might say to each other. And he found that he *didn't* enjoy putting animals in human dress or giving them umbrellas to carry or cars to drive. His characters, King-Smith decided, would be animals much like the ones he knew and loved, and his stories would be the kind that were both funny and real.

Leonard S. Marcus: What kind of child were you?

Dick King-Smith: I was a very lucky child, I now realize. I had a privileged early childhood. My brother was not born till I was nearly six years old, so for that time I was an "only" child, with all the family's attention focused on me.

My father's parents lived only about a mile away as the crow flies, and there were numerous uncles and aunts within visiting distance. Ours was a comfortable and quite large country house, with outbuildings and a big lawn and a good-sized garden and an orchard and a tennis court, and, as was the case in those days (I was born in 1922) for those who could afford it, I had, from an early age, a nanny to look after me, a nurse-maid, that is, who saw to all my needs.

I was an outgoing sort of child and made friends easily. I wasn't allowed a dog of my own till I was about nine. Prior to that, all the dogs in the house, usually three or four, belonged to Father or Mother, but my first dog was a mongrel called Peter. Though I was proud and fond of him, my chief loves were small pets. Father had a shed built with tiers of hutches in it, and here I kept guinea pigs and rabbits and mice.

Thinking back on it, I was still keeping guinea pigs in my fifties, and I even had a book published called *I Love Guinea Pigs*.

Q: What's the first time you can recall trying to make someone laugh?

A: At this remove I can't remember a particular first time, but I was certainly a little show-off who loved telling jokes and wanted to be the center of attention.

To be sure, she used a knife and fork and spoon, and afterward wiped her lips with a napkin while the rest cleaned their faces with their paws. But on occasion, so as not to seem standoffish, she would fill a bowl with milk and lap from it.

The Catlady

Q: Did you enjoy school?

A: School started very early, in that I had a governess, a family friend who came to our house to teach me. So I was fortunate enough to learn to read early, with all the enjoyment that that brings, and to write little stories at a young age. Then, at about seven, I was taken daily to a dame school (a school for young children, usually run by a woman). I especially remember it because, in between classes, we all went out to play, and our favorite game was Husbands and Wives, which meant that each little boy chose a little girl to be best friends with. I was the only one to have two wives, as I chose a pair of blond identical twins—Irene and Diana. Fancy, a bigamist at seven.

Then, at nine, I went off to what is known as a prep school, a boarding school taking boys up to about age thirteen. At which age I was moved to a public school, where I was educated until the age of eighteen. Here I didn't work as hard as I should have done, preferring acting in plays and generally playing the fool. I seem to remember I concocted a little show of my own, called, I think, "Bertie Bear Entertains." At one point the headmaster wrote in my report, "A public buffoon." My father was not best pleased, so I worked harder, and the following report stated, "Like a good horse, high-spirited and well-mannered." I had a mainly classical education, studying Latin and Greek at both schools, a line of learning that gave me an interest in words and their derivation, and in modes of expression. The fact that I was (and still am) hopelessly incompetent at anything mathematical led me to enjoy writing stories very much.

Dick King-Smith, age four, with Granny B. (far left), Great-Grandpa Heard, and his mother

Q: Were there good storytellers in your family?

A: Yes, one aunt in particular, and my father wasn't bad. My aunt Muriel (Father's sister) wrote a regular column for a woman's magazine. It was a series of stories about two little brothers with fair, curly hair, called Jeremy and John, who got up to all kinds of mischief, and believe it or not, its title was "Those Little Pickles."

Q: What would be an example of your granny B.'s sense of humor? Can you recall any of the jokes that your grandfathers liked to tell?

A: Granny B. was not a joke-teller, but she always saw the funny side of things, and she was a very happy person to be with. Grampy B. had been a very famous Rugby Union international footballer. He had been captain of Newport, and had been capped many times for Wales. I'm sure Granny B. had been very proud of him in those days, but I'm equally sure she would have been in fits of giggles at seeing his galloping about covered in mud. Though perhaps she never went to rugby matches. I never asked her. I wish I had.

Both my grandfathers were great punsters, and I'm very partial to a pun. A good pun, in my view, is one that most people would consider bad. I always remember a particular reported conversation between my King-Smith grandfather and his wife. He was about to set out on his bicycle (he was a keen cyclist) to a nearby suburb of Bristol by the name of Warmley. They called each other Potie and Motie:

Motie: Put your scarf on, Potie, and don't forget your gloves. The wind is cold.

>*Potie:* It's all right, Motie. I'm only going to Warmley, not Chile.

Q: Did the experience of World War II shape your feelings about life in some basic way?

>**A:** It showed me how precious life is. In the ten months that I served after the landing at Salerno, I lost so many friends as we fought our way north up Italy, and was eventually very lucky to survive when badly wounded south of Florence. Since that moment (5:30 a.m., July 12, 1944), every day I have lived has been a bonus.

Q: Did you go to the movies as a child? Listen to the radio? Were you much of a reader?

>**A:** I didn't listen to the radio much, but I liked going to the cinema, and I loved reading books, mainly books about animals, like *Winnie the Pooh* and *The Wind in the Willows,* and anything by Rudyard Kipling or Charles G. D. Roberts.

Q: Did humor help get you through the war?

>**A:** There's a lot of frontline soldiering that isn't in the least amusing, but it certainly helped to try and see the funny side of things whenever possible. Even a bad joke is better than nothing.

Q: How does writing compare with farming as a kind of work?

>**A:** There's really no comparison. The farming day contains so many set targets—the cows have to be milked morning and evening, the pigs and the poultry fed, the fields cultivated in

But in fact Aristotle managed to keep out of trouble for quite a
while. A whole week went by and the white kitten behaved sensibly.
He ate his meat and drank his milk and didn't scratch at the curtains
or the chair covers and didn't make any messes in the cottage.
Indeed by the end of that week Bella Donna had trained him to use
a dirt tray.
" You didn't make a very good start, Aristotle," she said to him,
" but now you're doing fine. Just keep on keeping out of mischief,"
and she crossed her long knobbly fingers.
If Aristotle had gone to an ordinary home, things might have been
different, but Bella's old cottage was in many ways a risky sort of
place for an adventurous kitten.
It stood in the middle of a little wood in which were many tall
trees, and through which flowed a swift steep-banked stream. On one
side of the wood there was a twisty road, and on the other a lofty
embankment along the top of which ran a railway line. There was also
a farm nearby on which lived a large fierce dog.
Aristotle's next adventure took place up a tall tree. Climbing was
something he found he rather liked, and he often now scrambled up
the creeper on the cottage walls and up the thatched roof to sit
upon the ridge-pole at the top (though he kept away from the chimney-
pot). He enjoyed this lofty perch but the cottage was quite a low
building and the trees around it were, he could see, much higher.
So one fine morning Aristotle chose a tall tree and leaped up its
trunk on to the lowest branch, and then on to a higher one, and so
on, up and up, feeling such a clever cat.
But the further up he went, the thinner and more springy the branches
became, till at last he found himself right at the top, clinging to
a thin bough that danced in the breeze, and he suddenly felt ever
such a scared kitten. The ground, he could see, was an awful long way

Manuscript page from *The Nine Lives of Aristotle*

their season. A writer's day is much more free and easy. If you can't think of a good idea, don't bother; things will work out when you're good and ready. What's more, you don't have to be young and strong—there's not much physical effort in using a Biro or tapping a typewriter.

Q: Why do you think you write so often about underdog characters?

A: I've always been in sympathy with the underdog. If you're at the bottom of the heap, the only way out is upwards. But it takes courage and persistence, which is why I enjoy the fun of making a less fortunate character become, eventually, top dog.

Q: Has an animal ever tried to make you laugh?

A: Yes, I know a parrot who never fails to make me laugh, and he *knows* when he makes a funny remark. You can see by the twinkle in his eye. I think that intelligent animals can, obviously, sometimes try to be amusing. I'm thinking of dogs and cats I've known, and of course of one of the brainiest creatures, a pig.

Q: What is the smartest thing you ever saw a pig do?

A: When I was farming, I had a wood in which my sows lived. On a freezing morning, after a bitterly cold night, I went out to look for a sow called Mollie, who I knew was close to farrowing. I walked through the frosty wood, getting more and more worried. Where was Mollie? Then at last I found her, under a big spreading tree that had given her cover, for it was the only frost-free part of the wood. At the base of it, she had made a huge warm nest of leaves. She got up to greet me, and there, snuggled down in the nest, were eight lovely little piglets.

Q: Why did you decide to write for children?

A: I couldn't possibly write a book for grown-ups. I'm not grown-up enough myself. Besides, an adult book would probably have to have sexy scenes in it, the sort of scenes that, when I read them, give me a fit of the giggles.

Q: Did you learn anything from the schoolchildren you taught that has helped you as a writer?

A: Yes. For most children, their story must have a good beginning, a good middle, and a good end. With luck, what I have thought up will interest them, excite them, maybe sometimes frighten them, but most importantly, I think, it must amuse them.

Q: Do you have a daily work routine?

A: I don't understand clever things like computers or word processors. I start about ten in the morning, sitting in my little study in my very old cottage (about 375 years old), scribbling away—sometimes very slowly—with a Biro. But before I get out my ancient typewriter, in the afternoon, I try to make the scribble as fault-free as I can, because I type out each bit with one finger and I don't want to have to do that twice. Between ten in the morning and about four in the afternoon, I might, if all goes well, have done a chapter.

Q: What do you tell young people who say they want to write?

A: I tell them to read lots of books, good ones, not rubbish. That way they'll pick up a bit of how writers put things together, of the style they use. I don't ask them to copy other people's ideas. But the more a child reads and the more enjoyment he or she gets from the reading, the more each child will find a style of their own. I also say, "Show your stories to other people, your mum, your dad, your teacher, and listen to their opinions of them."

Q: What is the best thing about being a writer?

A: I've written a lot of books since my first one, *The Fox Busters*, which was published in 1978. I've lost count of the number, probably over a hundred. Many millions of

"But I'm not a sheepdog either," said Babe, and he scrambled up the stack of straw bales and looked over the bars.

"You see?" he said.

"Well I'll be dipped," said the old sheep, peering up at him. "No more you ain't. What are you?"

"Pig," said Babe. "Large White. What are you?"

"Ewe," said the sheep.

"No, not me, you—what are you?"

"I'm a ewe."

Mum was right, thought Babe, they certainly are stupid. But if I'm going to learn how to be a sheep-pig I must try to understand them, and this might be a good chance.

Babe: The Gallant Pig

copies have been sold all over the world, and some of my books have been translated into many—perhaps twenty—other languages. Some of my stories have been adapted for television, and one, *The Sheep-Pig,* was made into a film called *Babe.* More recently, another book, *The Water Horse,* was made into a film. So there's quite a lot of money coming my way, which is nice for my very large family and me. Money may not be the most important thing in life, but you're a silly billy if you don't like it. Another nice thing is when critics write in a newspaper or magazine that they think one of my books is good.

But the single nicest thing about having been a children's writer for twenty-nine years is the tens of thousands of letters that I get all the time from young readers all over the world, telling me they've enjoyed this book or that (and every letter gets an answer). After a number of different careers, none of them very successful, I've found myself in the business of giving pleasure to a great many children. I'm a lucky man.

A DICK KING-SMITH READER

Babe: The Gallant Pig, illustrated by Mary Raynor (Crown, 1988)

An autobiography:

> *Chewing the Cud: An Extraordinary Life Remembered by the Author of Babe: The Gallant Pig* (Knopf, 2002)

The Cuckoo Child, illustrated by Leslie Bowman (Hyperion, 1993)

The Fox Busters, illustrated by Jon Miller (Delacorte, 1978)

Harry's Mad, illustrated by Jill Bennett (Crown, 1984)

I Love Guinea Pigs, illustrated by Anita Jeram (Candlewick, 1995)

Martin's Mice, illustrated by Jez Alborough (Crown, 1988)

Mr. Ape, illustrated by Roger Roth (Crown, 1998)

Mr. Potter's Pet, illustrated by Mark Teague (Hyperion, 1996)

The Nine Lives of Aristotle, illustrated by Bob Graham (Candlewick, 2003)

The School Mouse, illustrated by Cynthia Fisher (Hyperion, 1995)

The Terrible Trins, illustrated by Mark Teague (Crown, 1994)

The Toby Man, illustrated by Lynette Hemmant (Crown, 1989)

The Water Horse, illustrated by David Parkins (Knopf, 1998)

HILARY MCKAY

Born 1959, Boston, Lincolnshire, England

Hilary McKay's keen sense of modesty is such that on most days she would probably rather talk about anyone more than about herself. For her, better still than to talk at all is to listen intently to the things other people say, and to the precise *way* they say them—a penchant for which she seems to have been given specially fine-tuned equipment. For McKay, listening is strongly linked to another favorite activity—reading—which she learned to do at the age of four and which remains, she says, as ever-present a part of her life as the weather. Asked once why she began writing books, she replied that perhaps it was simply because she had already read so many.

McKay grew up as the eldest of four sisters in a sleepy river town set down "a long way from anywhere" in the flatlands north of London. Her family background was one of striking contrasts. Her father's father was a chimney sweep and a colorful figure beloved by the local community into which she was born. Her mother's proudly "posh" family was sedate and rich. During the years of her childhood, McKay's parents had little money, rode bicycles around town instead of a car, and for entertainment looked to the local library and to the stories they told one another.

"Is it true?" is a question young Hilary learned not to ask, especially with regard to her father's outlandish yarns, many of them supposedly tales about their own relatives. McKay inherited her father's knack for spinning bits and pieces of memory and imagination into tales of family life that are both witty and wise. "That," she says, "is what my family do to stories. Leave them, not as they were, but as they would wish to find them."

Leonard S. Marcus: What kind of child were you?

> **Hilary McKay:** I was a very thick child. I thought our teachers were there in school because they loved us all. But then it dawned on me that they got paid to teach us.
>
> My sisters and I all got a little labeled at school. We were

considered "different." I think that was because we didn't have TVs at home, and television was the language of children. My parents were and are both avid readers. They had the idea that if their children watched TV, they wouldn't read. So they got rid of all that sort of thing. Radio wasn't allowed either.

Q: Did you like school anyway?

A: No, because there wasn't anything that I did well there. I didn't fit in until the last two years.

Q: Did you enjoy reading?

A: Oh, yes! We read Lucy Maud Montgomery. We read E. Nesbit over and over again. I remember saying, "I'm bored," and my father saying, "Read a book." We had a very good town library. I don't remember a librarian. We were just let loose in this huge, wood-paneled room that was stuffed with books. I remember being desperate to be fourteen when you could get books from the adult library because, after a time, I had finished the children's library.

Q: Were there good storytellers in your family?

A: My father was a very funny, brilliant storyteller. He liked the classics and would adapt them for us. Every year, when he told Dickens's *A Christmas Carol*, he would have us choose the presents for Bob Cratchit's sledge and would have us wondering what Mrs. Cratchit was going to do with that huge turkey that had been landed on her on Christmas morning. We'd think, *She'll* never *get it cooked in time for lunch.* He made it all very personal.

At times, my father was *too* good a storyteller. Everyone's parents perpetuate Father Christmas, things like that. We had a few extras thrown in. For years my father, and my mother too, had us convinced that we had two older brothers in Australia. It's tempting for parents to carry jokes too far, because children are so gullible. I've been tempted. But this joke upset my parents in the end when my littlest sister wrote about the brothers in school, and the teacher asked, "What happened to the boys?"

Q: There's a picture of you at about the age of eight standing in Trafalgar Square with a pigeon on your head.

A: I remember that. That pigeon was very heavy on my head. It was not a fun experience. But going to London, which was a once-yearly family treat, was always exciting, with all the Underground trains and things.

Q: When you were ten you had a teacher with the perfect name for a teacher: Mrs. Rule.

A: She was a lovely, gentle woman, and a wonderful teacher. She read aloud to us every day and she was very good at it. She would pick out individual children and the things they were good at or interested in, and make it matter. She was a star, really. She would play ten minutes of classical music every day. "Sit and listen to this!" I remember her bringing in a tortoise on my birthday because I liked animals. It walked around the classroom all day. She made us write books on Friday afternoons. "Write a book on whatever you're really interested in." She used to stagger in with piles of reference books for us. That was when I wrote my *Natural History of the World*.

Q: Would you say that was your first book?

A: Yes, that was my first book. Mrs. Rule commented on every page, and did the same for all thirty of us.

Q: Was it that experience that gave you the idea to become a writer?

A: No. It never occurred to me that I *could* become one. In fact, I didn't like writing stories in school very much, although I liked reading them.

Q: Later you studied botany and zoology and went to work in a chemistry lab. Do you think that your science training and work helped in some way to prepare you to become a writer?

A: I think so. If you work in a laboratory, you have deadlines that are in hours and days. So it keeps you awake. It keeps you noticing details. But I was always aware of people around me.

Q: Can you picture Mrs. Rule now?

A: She had chestnut curly hair, very shiny, and there was a rumor going around among the boys—which wasn't true— that it was a wig. It *wasn't* a wig. But it used to be a thing to walk up close enough to her to see the joinings. She was tall and was always beautifully made up and beautifully dressed. She made being at school feel like an occasion. She didn't really look like she fit into a grubby little 1960s classroom, but she did. Her lipstick was very red, which must have been the fashion. Her dog was called the Black Panther, after *The Jungle Book*, which she'd read to us. She was very adventurous, and she loved maps—which made us all love maps. Once we measured the circumference of the earth using the shadows found in the playground.

Q: Tell me about your college friend, Isabel.

A: Isabel was an English student when I was a zoology student. Because her lectures were all in the early morning, before mine began, she would say, "Come with me!" And so I got into books I would never have read—Early English and Anglo-Saxon literature.

Isabel and I have always written proper letters to each other, and once when I was in one of my miserable laboratory jobs, she said to me, "Well, if you can write letters, I should think you can write a book." I thought, *I'll see if I can!* I had never stopped reading children's books, and I tried to write the kind of book that I would have enjoyed when I was nine or ten.

Q: Why a children's book, though?

A: Because they're shorter! I was working full-time, so I don't think I was going to write a long book. I wrote a short one to see what would happen, and I was lucky that it was published.

Q: How did the Casson family take shape in your mind?

A: I really don't know where they came from. There is perhaps a little of me in Eve, also something of a good friend of mine who does not like to cook—and whose children are all perfectly healthy anyway. Originally, there was only going to be one book. I had a dream about the garden that I wrote about in *Saffy's Angel.* That was very helpful! As for the rest, you put the things that interest you in the books you write: stars,

> Darling Daddy,
>
> This is Rose.
>
> Very good news. Caddy is going to marry Michael. In case you have forgotten because you have not been home for so long he is the one with the ponytail and the earring that you do not like. But we do. And Caddy says she will have a white lace dress and three brides-maids . . . and a big party for everyone. . . . Saffron said That will cost a few weeks housekeeping and Mummy said Yes but we do not need to worry about that. Daddy will pay.
>
> Love, Rose.
>
> *Indigo's Star*

natural history, Arthurian legends, art . . . If I know a little bit about a thing, I'll use it.

Q: Has being a parent influenced your writing in some way?

A: I try not to overprotect our children. We're lucky that we live in a little village and I can let our children loose to go around by themselves. There are a lot of children here in England, and I suppose in America too, who are driven around everywhere and have an adult always in the background. It's very hard to write about them, because they're so supervised. I think that's why so many people write fantasy. In the old days, you could get rid of the adults in the first paragraph by saying they're all going camping, or to India, or something like that—as E. Nesbit did. But now children have adults peering down their necks at all times. So, it's very hard, in a realistic story, to let the children do anything adventurous. I remember having Rose go up a stepladder and being told by an editor, "I'm sorry, but you can't have Rose do that, because children might copy her and fall off."

Q: Does writing about a family of artists like the Cassons give you a way around that problem? With their father away in London most of the time and their mother busy painting in her shed, the children are often left to their own devices.

A: Absolutely. I get lots of mail from children. Many write to me and say, "I wish we had that family."

Q: Still, things aren't all wonderful at Banana House. When Rose paints a mural of her family, she shows everyone gathered on the deck of a sinking ark. The scene could be a cross between the stories of Noah's Ark and the Titanic.

A: Well, Rose is very dismissive of her family. She is a tough little girl, but I think she's also quite vulnerable as well, actually. She speaks her own mind, as I think most children do.

Q: You even make a point of having Rose say that she thinks reading is a huge waste of time.

A: She's very confident about her painting. That's *her* way to express herself for now. I don't think I judge people in my books, or in my life.

I go to a school every Friday to work with the children, and

I find that boys are far harder to get reading than the girls, on the whole. I work with the ones who won't read with anybody else at the moment. The teachers haven't given up, but they want a new approach. I'm a novelty to them—though I suppose the novelty will wear off in a year or two! I take them out of class to the library in twos and fours, and we build dens on the floor with the big floor cushions, and they are lions in the den, and they read to the monkeys—just anything to get them turning the pages. It's quite nice, really.

Q: It must be enjoyable to return in book after book to the same family of characters, to see how they're doing and how they'll change.

A: I have gotten very fond of the Cassons. I'm very protective of them.

At the time I was writing *Saffy's Angel*, I already knew an awful lot of the Cassons' backstory, and so it was quite easy to pick another character and move a bit forward in *Indigo's Star*. The characters took over quite a lot themselves. I don't know how that happens, but I would hear their voices, and at times I would almost stop using my imagination and just listen.

Q: What about the Cassons most appeals to you?

A: Well, if you think about it, the children are loved. As I mentioned before, I know a particular mother who hates cooking. She never cooks, but she loves her children. They feel confident in their talents. Nobody puts them down. I fought this battle for a long time. Am I writing about abused children? No, I'm not! I know abused children. I've seen them and met them. They're the ones who are frightened at the world. The Cassons

First, p126
Oh dear, I think you have spotted a big mistake here—
I have made Caddy lose a year of University. To straighten it out

therefore:
1. This story must take place the year after Caddy finishes, which is a whole year after the end of Permanent Rose.

2. Therefore, the September that Rose goes into Miss Farley's class (The Flying Feeling story) she is nine going on ten. The following June, when Caddy's wedding takes place she would still be nine, and still in Miss Farley's class, so that is okay, but the birthday she refers to, when Michael goes away, is her ninth. ie she is remembering a long time back.

3. This means that a) by the time Caddy and Alex get married (or try to) Michael has been away for a year and nine months, and Caddy has been out of University for a year, which I think gives her time for most of her jobs.

To make this work in the text we need to put in the following changes:

P140
"A pity you could not marry him yourself," remarked Kiran once, a long time ago, when all this first happened.

p141
"Right now, Michael is away with his friend Luke. They are travelling on motorbikes round Europe. This is Luke's way of

E-mail mesage from Hilary McKay to her American editor as work progressed on *Caddy Ever After*

curing Michael's broken heart. They have been gone for ages, more than a year, so I know it has not worked.

I am ten now. That is how long it has been. Michael went away just before my ninth birthday.

I had not seen him for a while, and then one Saturday, about a week before he left, he turned up. He came specially to see me."

p141 (further down)
"There would be the lovely coldness in the air that makes running easier than walking. Daddy would come home and measure my height on the kitchen wall and be amazed at how much I'd grown like he always does on my birthday."

"Do you think I've got much taller this summer?" I asked Michael.

"Much," said Michael. "First thing I noticed when I saw you. What do you want for your birthday?"

p144
"That was the Autumn that I was nine, and now more than a year has gone by, and it is summer again. Caddy finished University ages ago. Michael and Luke are still not home.

The last thing Michael said to me was, "Don't let Caddy marry anyone else while I'm gone!"

P.134 key stage 2
Just take it out, so that the text reads

". . . Ere we resume our exile in the brain numbing wastes of Literacy Hour . . ."

I hope this works Karen,
yours Hilary

> Then she and her father walked home together, Bill striding along as if he owned the town, Rose hopping and skipping beside him, as temporarily happy as she had ever been in her life.
>
> "I loved your letters," said Bill.
>
> "Did you?"
>
> "Made me laugh out loud."
>
> "They weren't meant to make you laugh."
>
> "Oh. What were they meant to do?"
>
> "Make you come home," said Rose.
>
> *Indigo's Star*

aren't like that. Their problems aren't that "Mommy is scary" or "Nobody cares about me." Their background, whatever else it has done to them, has made them think, *I'm an OK sort of person*. Somebody in the house will always listen to them, and nobody is pressuring them like a lot of children are being pressured to be better or brighter or to learn to dance or play an instrument. I hope it's a positive view of children.

Q: Tom's grandmother says, "There are all sorts of families and most of them seem to get on together, one way or the other." And Sarah says, with what sounds like envy, "You Cassons are so artistic and dysfunctional and cool. It's not fair."

A: Well, Sarah has another kind of life.

Q: She turns out to be something of a rebel—when she tricks her parents into taking Saffy along to Italy.

A: Not a rebel. But I didn't want her to be a "girl in a wheelchair." I wanted her to be a person.

Q: The Cassons' story has the makings of a darkly serious book: an absent father; a little girl, Rose, who is furious with him; a mother who's easily and often distracted; a boy, Indigo, who has lots of fears . . . Yet there's so much to laugh at. How did you manage to pull that off?

A: I've always listened closely to people, and I think if you listen to what people say, *exactly* as they say it, and write it down, it's pretty nearly always funny. I don't know why that is. I think the way people talk is part of their character, and if you just write it down with no frills, no comments on it yourself, it strikes home with people, and they laugh because they recognize it. If you were to write down the average child's classroom conversation, you'd find something to smile at, because it's fairly blunt and fairly direct.

Q: What else do children write to you?

A: Some say, "I have a father like that," or "I have a mother like that." I received a letter from a lovely girl who said she

> Bill did guilt as beautifully as he did everything else.
>
> *Permanent Rose*

had recorded two books of mine—on a karaoke machine. I thought, *Oh, no!* But she did it so beautifully that I showed it to my publisher and we ended up in a recording studio in London, where she did a proper recording, which we used as publicity for *Caddy Ever After*. It was a good confidence-building thing for her, and it gave her a few days in London.

Q: Do you have a work routine?

A: I try to be very disciplined, but I'm not really what you'd call a full-time writer. I have two children, and I go into schools a lot. I write in between. I generally write in the morning, and I generally write at nighttime. There are times when I'll do anything *not* to write, when I'd rather clean my son's footballer boots than write a book.

Q: How much do you know about a book from the start?

A: I usually have the beginning and know how a book is going to end. I often don't know how I'll get to the end, or if I think I do know, it does not work out. I'll look back at my early notes and find it's a different story.

Q: Do you read your work aloud as you write it?

A: Over and over again, *more* than I write it: to get the rhythm just right and to get it to scan. I do that all the time.

Q: How do you know when a book is done?

A: Sometimes an editor has to come here to my home and pry a manuscript loose from me.

A HILARY McKAY READER

The Casson Family books:

> *Saffy's Angel* (Margaret K. McElderry/Simon and Schuster, 2002)
>
> *Indigo's Star* (Margaret K. McElderry/Simon and Schuster, 2004)
>
> *Permanent Rose* (Margaret K. McElderry/Simon and Schuster, 2005)
>
> *Caddy Ever After* (Margaret K. McElderry/Simon and Schuster, 2006)
>
> *Forever Rose* (Margaret K. McElderry/Simon and Schuster, 2008)

The Conroy Sisters books:

> *The Exiles* (Margaret K. McElderry/Atheneum, 1992)
>
> *The Exiles at Home* (Margaret K. McElderry/Simon and Schuster, 1994)
>
> *The Exiles in Love* (Margaret K. McElderry/Simon and Schuster, 1998)

From: Daniel Pinkwater
To: Leonard S. Marcus
Sent: Mon, 16 Jul 2007 1:09 pm
Subject: Re: interview bk

Dear Dr. Marcus —

I'm afraid I can't be of any help to you with your project. Your letter
suggests that you want to interview funny writers. I am not funny.
I am just misunderstood. Anyway, 1. there are too many demands
on my time, 2. I will be out of the country, 3. I am telephobic, and
4. I'm not interested. Good luck with your book, which promises to
be Captain Billy's Whiz-Bang for the 21st century.

Daniel Pinkwater

P.S. If you are a completeness-freak you have my permission
to include this email in place of the one- or two-hour telephone
interview you sadistically suggest.

LOUIS SACHAR

Born 1954, East Meadow, New York

L ouis Sachar speaks in the unhurried, probing manner of a man hoping to surprise himself. This, it turns out, is also the way he writes a book: with no definite plan other than to have no plan, and with maybe a character or two in mind in whom he senses the makings of a good story.

Nearly every character about whom Sachar's hunches have proven correct has been an outsider figure of one kind or another, a young person—like Bradley in *There's a Boy in the Girls' Bathroom*, Angeline in *Someday Angeline*, and Gary in *Dogs Don't Tell Jokes*—who, try as they may, have great difficulty fitting in with their fellow schoolmates, family, or world. In real life, an outsider is bound to face some lonely, unfunny times, as Sachar himself learned over a stretch of years when he was lumped in with the "uncool" kids at school. As a writer he has an amazing knack for getting inside the skins of young people with similar troubles and for finding a light side in the dark dilemma of being different. In doing so, Sachar bears out the truth of the old saying that "laughter is the best medicine"—but only, as he shows time and again, when we're laughing with and not at one another.

Leonard S. Marcus: What kind of child were you?

Louis Sachar: I was a pretty happy child, a pretty good student at school. I liked playing Little League. I played infield. I had lots of friends through sixth grade. Then in middle school I went through a lot of the problems that people go through at that age. Suddenly I was on the outs, not cool anymore, and the kids who had been my friends were hanging out with the cool guys. It took a while for me to find myself again. I write about that now because I lived through it, and I see it happening to lots and lots of kids.

Q: Did you enjoy reading?

A: I ordered books at school from the Scholastic book club and I'd read them, but they didn't do much for me. It wasn't until I was in high school and read J. D. Salinger, Kurt Vonnegut, and

Little League second baseman Louis Sachar, age seven or eight

Dostoyevsky that I thought, *Wow, this is great!* A friend and I both read Salinger's *Nine Stories* on our own. We would read each story separately and then discuss it, trying to figure out what it meant.

Q: You were very good at math in school. Your character Angeline in *Someday Angeline* says she thinks that algebra is funny. Did you think so too?

A: Not funny, but I thought of it as a game, a puzzle. I never thought of algebra as work.

Q: Do you see a connection between what goes into doing math and what is involved in writing a story?

A: There's a twisted mathematical logic to *Sideways Stories from Wayside School* in the fact, for instance, that there's no nineteenth story but it's a thirty-story building. I can't tell you how often kids have said to me, "How can it be thirty stories if there's no nineteenth? Doesn't that make it twenty-nine?" They're just insistent upon it. There's the story about Joe counting. He counts wrong and gets the right answers. He counts right and gets the wrong answers. Even in the stories that don't involve numbers, things have a logical conclusion or the conclusion is a logical build-up of illogic. That's part of the humor in the book.

I play a lot of bridge, which is a logical-puzzle game, and one of my bridge-playing friends told me that she thought the story of *Holes* unfolds with the logic of a bridge hand. When you play a hand of bridge, you think it all out beforehand and then you follow a logical path that leaves you at the end in the position where you want to be. There is something in my writing that is more math- or logic-based than most writing.

Q: You worked as a lawyer before you became a full-time writer, and in *Dogs Don't Tell Jokes* your character Gus finds a law school diploma in the trash one day. I was wondering if that diploma was, in a sense, yours?

A: I think I *was* thinking of that as mine when I wrote about it, or the equivalent of mine. I never exactly threw my diploma away, though.

I wrote my first book, *Sideways Stories from Wayside School*, right out of college. I was sending it out to publishers around the same time that I was sending out applications to law school. I was accepted to law school, and during my first week at school I heard from a publisher who wanted to publish my book. So I was always ambivalent about law and about whether

I wanted to finish law school or try to make a living as a writer. My love was for writing, of course. But even after I started to get published, I didn't know if I would ever make any money at it. So I continued law school, passed the bar, and then went looking for a job. But I never really looked very hard, and every night I'd come home and worry about it and think, *God, tomorrow I've got to get serious about looking for a job!* This went on for four years.

Finally after four years I just told myself, *Quit worrying about it. I've obviously made a decision not to be a lawyer and I should stick with it.* That was around the time I wrote *Dogs Don't Tell Jokes.* Even then, I did part-time legal work for another four years before quitting altogether.

Q: In *Wayside School Is Falling Down*, Myron meets a man in the school basement who tells him, "Do you want to be free, or do you want to be safe? . . . You can't have it both ways."

A: That's right. He's talking about the same thing.

> "Did you say there was a girl named Bebe Gunn?" asked Ray.
>
> "Yes," said Allison. "Bebe's a very good artist."
>
> "My name is Gunn, too," said Ray. "I wonder if we're related."
>
> *Wayside School Is Falling Down*

Q: Were there good storytellers in your family?

A: Not storytellers. But my brother, who's three years older than I am, was always a good writer and reader. He's never published anything, but he was probably the biggest influence on me. I never felt in competition with my brother. I always admired him. He is very much a non-conformist and happy with who he is. He is good at not letting society dictate how he lives his life, at resisting the pressure to wear a tie or get a job. All his ex-girlfriends are still his friends, and not too many people can say that. A lot of things that the rest of society does just don't make sense to him. It seems to me that he has a very healthy outlook on life.

Q: In *Dogs Don't Tell Jokes*, when Mrs. Snitzberry is explaining to Gary why she doesn't mind having jokes told about her by Goon, she says, "Humor is man's greatest gift." When she says this to Gary, are you also saying it to the reader?

A: I think it is more true for Gary than it is for me. For Gary, humor is the ultimate thing. Mrs. Snitzberry is more or less a figment of Gary's imagination.

Q: Why did you want to write that book?

A: A lot of things go into choosing what book to write. I started *Dogs Don't Tell Jokes* because I really liked the characters I had created in *Someday Angeline*. That book hadn't sold very well or gotten much recognition, so I wanted to give the characters a second chance.

My first book, *Sideways Stories,* was originally published by a small publisher based in Chicago. People who read the book seemed to love it, but the publisher wasn't able to get it to a lot of readers. Then the company went out of business, and my book was out of print for a while.

There's a Boy in the Girls' Bathroom was my first book to do really well. Then *Sideways Stories* was republished, and I became known for those two books. I began then to feel that after years of struggling to see if I could make it as a children's book writer, I'd finally succeeded. Gary's story is about struggling too—struggling to try and write jokes, and about feeling at times that everything he wrote was stupid. Those are the same feelings that I would go through when I was writing a book. I remember that as I was writing *Dogs Don't Tell Jokes,* I wasn't sure how it was going to end—whether or not Gary was going to flop at the school talent show. It wasn't until I got to the end, and I thought about all the work he had put into it, that I realized that it seemed right that Gary should succeed.

Q: The ending is beautiful, and mysterious. From his place on the school auditorium stage, Gary suddenly notices that the theater curtain is worn and shabby—an imperfect, human thing. Then, after having just made everybody in the audience laugh he starts to cry. Why did you choose to end the story that way?

A: I think it's because during the time that Gary was suffering, when people would make fun of him, he would always laugh it off. Laughing was his defense mechanism. Now when he'd succeeded and had done what he wanted to do, everything was reversed. So he starts to cry. Noticing the curtain is about showing how into the moment he is, taking in everything.

Q: Earlier in the book, the teacher in charge of the talent show, Miss Langley, tells Gary not to get his hopes up too high about winning because (as she puts it) telling jokes "isn't exactly a talent—like singing, or playing the piano, or even *bird calls.*"

> A: Comic writers are often told the same thing. Even though it takes a lot of work and talent to write good comedy, people seem to think it's just a joke.
>
> There are a lot of different kinds of comedy. Some of it is funny for the moment but doesn't linger. You get the feeling that the writer wasn't taking it seriously, *So why should I?* It's often the comedy that disturbs—Kurt Vonnegut's books for instance—that is thought of as literature.

Q: Of all the outsider characters you've written about, is there one you feel closest to?

> A: Probably David in *The Boy Who Lost His Face.* Like me, he was someone who in middle school suddenly lost his old friends and was struggling with making new ones.

Q: Bradley, the outsider in *There's a Boy in the Girls' Bathroom,* starts out being such a sad character. How did you find the humor in his story?

> A: Well, my first instinct is to write humorously. I got the idea for that book from a friend of mine who told me about having moved and started fifth grade in a new school. Like Jeff in the book, the teacher had brought him to the front of the room, introduced him to the class, and assigned him a seat. Then one of the kids said to him, "Don't sit there. No one likes sitting next to"—in his case it was a boy named Donny. Then the teacher, in front the whole class, acknowledged that what the student had said was true by saying, "Sorry, Jeff. Nobody likes to sit next to Donny." My friend was so amazed that a teacher

could be that insensitive. After hearing about the incident, I began writing the book.

So then I was making up things for Bradley to do to show why nobody liked sitting next to him. It was just natural to me to make those things funny. Bradley will say something outlandish or impossible about himself and end with, "Call my mom if you don't believe me," or "Call the zoo if you don't believe me." Each time he does this, you say to yourself, on one level, *Poor kid.* But at the same time, it's funny.

It's hard to say why I write certain things. A lot of times, I feel almost like I'm in a hypnotic state. I'm just *there.* I'm there with the character, feeling what he's feeling, seeing what he's seeing. I was there with Gary when in the last scene of *Dogs Don't Tell Jokes* he suddenly saw the curtain.

Q: Did you ever want to be a stand-up comic yourself?

A: No. I'm much happier writing, not being out in public. There was a time when I used to crack jokes a lot, but they would always land kind of flat. One of the nice things about writing is that you get to rewrite—and take back all the stupid things you said. I felt I had an easy path when I was writing *Dogs Don't Tell Jokes,* because if something I wrote was funny, well, great. And if it wasn't funny, I was still showing Gary making up a stupid, silly joke.

Q: Why did you decide to write for young readers at all?

A: While I was in college, I worked for a time as an elementary school teacher's aide for an hour a day. After a while I was hired to be the noontime supervisor—the person who passed out the balls on the playground and kept the kids from killing

What do you think of the title:

Dogs Don't Tell Jokes.

December 21, 1990

Dear Frances,

Enclosed is the revised manuscript, but you already know that.

A lot of what Gary goes through in preparing his act are the same things that I go through in writing. Something seems funny to me one day, then the next day it doesn't. Or it reads well one day, the next day it doesn't. And suddenly I'll remember something I threw away and decide it will fit perfectly. So, as always, all my changes are open for discussion.

I know you meant it as a joke, but you are definitely not a censor. I don't know if you realize how much I value your comments.

beginning.

Stupid grin: You asked at one point if I wanted the smile printed on the page. Yes, I did. I like the idea of Gary smiling stupidly up at the reader. Unfortunately it is only used at the ~~building.~~ I put it in places where the point of view suddenly shifts. Perhaps we need to find places to use it throughout the manuscript. It doesn't have to be my drawing. Somebody from the art department can probably do it better. It should be very simple.

I've removed all but one of the footnotes-- Page 26, although it doesn't have to appear at the foot of the page.

please

As suggested by one of the "book reports", I've added a little more of Gary trying ~~to be like~~ Joe. I've set the date of the talent show back from Thursday to Friday.

I've re-written the scene with Mrs. Snitzberry. I'm reluctant to take it out. I think it's sharper now, and I also think it's more effective after the new material showing Gary trying to fit in.

I have several ideas about restructuring the first couple of chapters, along with, as one of your readers suggested, presenting the episode from page 43 earlier in the book. I'd like to talk them over with you. These are the ideas:

1. Move the episode from page 43 to the end of chapter 1.

2. Delete the "editorializing" at the end of chapter 2, and put the episode from page 43 there, right after the newspaper article.

3. Same as above, but also combine first two chapters. (I mention this because I found when I read aloud to groups I always went right into the second chapter without even acknowledging a

Letter from Louis Sachar to his editor, Frances Foster, outlining some of the changes he made in the revised manuscript for *Dogs Don't Tell Jokes* new chapter. My initial reason for making the first couple of chapters so short was that since this is all background material, and I didn't want to bore the reader.

    4. Leave episode from page 43 on page 43.

    My inclination now is to go with option # 3. But as of now I have not renumbered the chapters.

Page 20. (He also had a dictionary, a book called <u>Sideways</u> <u>Arithmetic</u> <u>From</u> <u>Wayside</u> <u>School</u>, which he didn't understand, and a novel...etc.)

    Is this still too self serving? I'm constantly hearing from kids who tell me they don't understand that book. They may appreciate the author's recognition that the book is difficult, and that Gary has trouble with the book too. For those who haven't read the book, they should just pass over it without being distracted.

Page 34. In <u>Someday Angeline</u>, Mr. Bone had a "Save The Whales" sticker on her car. Her remark about recycling here is just to continue that aspect of her character, but I don't want it to sound preachy. Does it still stick out as preachy as it now reads? I also like the juxtapostion of real problems (destruction of the enviornment) against Gary's trivial problem (Nobody laughs at his jokes) even though it really isn't done enough to leave much of an impression.

Pages 42-47. Now that I've moved the old page 43 up in the book, this chapter has somewhat of a hole. I've re-written it a little bit trying to fill the hole, but it isn't as strong as it was. Perhaps the old page 43 should be left here after all. What do you think? I probably wouldn't be so worried about it if you hadn't written "good chapter" at the end of it.

I broke chapter nine into two chapters. I was bothered by the transition from Gary's first day without telling jokes to suddenly a summary of his first week.

After having done the above, I think it's effective to combine the old chapter ten with the new chapter ten.

I've given some thought to allowing Angeline come to the talent show after all. I chose not to do it, but I'm not sure if that decision is based on artistic reasons, or if it's because I'm leaving for Texas in two days, and I want to get this done before I go.

I no longer think there is a factual problem with why Angeline can't make it. See pages 30 and 92-93 each other. I loved it. It was so refreshing to spend time with these bright-eyed, joy-filled kids. So I thought about trying to write a children's book. *Wayside Stories* took me a year to write. It was another couple of years before it was published.

Q: Who is the teacher, Judy Allen, who shares the dedication in *Holes*?

A: She was my daughter's fifth-grade teacher. My daughter learned a lot from her about how to be a better person—more than anything about self-confidence.

Q: So your daughter's teacher was the opposite of the adults in *Holes*, the warden, for instance.

A: Oh, yeah. Definitely.

Q: Do you revise your work?

A: I do six or seven drafts.

Q: How did *Holes* change?

A: It's hard to remember, but I'll begin by saying that when I start a book, I don't make a plan. I don't know where I'm going with it. I just try to find something that intrigues me enough to write about it for at least a week. With *Holes* I began with the camp. That came out of the fact that I had recently moved from San Francisco to Texas, where it's so hot in summer and summer lasts forever. I was writing about the heat. Lake Travis is not too far from Austin, and I imagined it being so hot that Lake Travis dried up.

Every other book I'd written had been about kids at school, and I was tired of doing that and was trying to come up with something else, something bigger than my other books, which are introspective studies of a character like Gary or Bradley or Angeline. I wanted to make this a big adventure book. I got the idea for a juvenile correction camp before I had any characters. And I had Stanley's great-great-grandfather before I ever got to Stanley. So there I was, writing about this character who I referred to as Stanley's great-great-grandfather without ever telling who Stanley was. I think that's how I began.

Once I had the camp and the boys, I had them digging holes. I knew they would find some buried treasure. And I made up that the treasure had been buried by someone named Kissin' Kate Barlow. At first, I didn't know who she was, or how I was going to use her. I just thought of her as a colorful character. And I made up the deadly lizards, again just trying at first to add color to the story.

So then I had six characters, was making up the story, and was trying to see where it would go. I often don't finish a first draft. I got about two-thirds of the way through my first draft of *Holes,* as far as Stanley and Zero going up to God's Thumb. At the time it wasn't onions they were surviving on, but nuts and berries. I had been thinking at the beginning that the warden was going to be related to Kissin' Kate Barlow, that she was going to be her granddaughter. And the whole thing with the poison nail polish . . . I was thinking that maybe Kate Barlow had had poison lipstick, so that it sort of ran in the family. Then when I got to the point of writing about Kate and had to decide who she was and how that treasure got there, suddenly Kate became a very likable, heroic, tragic character. That seemed to come out of nowhere. Much to my surprise, I suddenly liked her a lot. She's actually my favorite character in the book. Because of that, I changed it so that Trout Walker was related to the warden.

Q: Why is Kate your favorite?

A: Because her relationship with Sam is such a moving, powerful one. It was almost as if that story was told to me. It too seemed to come out of nowhere. I remember thinking, *Who is she?* She wasn't always a criminal. What did she start out as, then? How about as a schoolteacher? So then I had to figure out what would lead this schoolteacher to become a criminal, and then I thought it might have something to do with the story about Sam.

Q: You say in the book that Kate "died laughing."

A: Well, that was part of her being such a bigger-than-life, colorful character. Maybe she knew that by her death she was sentencing Trout to a life of digging holes in search of buried treasure.

That was the first draft. By the second draft I had the onions and I finished it. I remember I was pretty excited when I got the idea that the lizards actually protect the kids from the warden when they're in the holes and also that it's the onions that keep the lizards from biting them. *Great!* I thought. *I just love it!*

By the third draft I basically had the whole story and it was a matter of figuring out how to interweave all the different threads: the story of Kate, the story of Stanley's great-great-grandfather, and so on, so that the reader can learn about all of them without having to ask, "Why are we reading about this now?" The question I'm usually asked is, "How did you get everything to tie together so neatly at the end?" But that wasn't the hard part. I *knew* how it would all fit together. The hard part was figuring out how to place all those stories throughout the novel in a way that would flow for the reader.

Q: When did you choose the title?

A: At the very end. I remember not being real sure of it, telling people, "Well, I think I'm calling it *Holes.*" I'd come up with a second title: *Wrong Time, Wrong Place, Wrong Kid.* My daughter liked that one better. *Holes* seemed more serious. Then I'd be speaking at a school or a convention and I'd say to the audience, "I have this new book coming out called *Holes,*" and people would say back, "Called *what?*" The *h* sound is hard to project. So I would have to repeat it: *Holes*—you know, *H-O-L-E-S.*" I'm still not sure if it is a good title or not.

Q: There's a moment near the end of *Holes* that reminds me of the last scene in *Dogs Don't Tell Jokes.* It's when Stanley is still in the hole surrounded by lizards and thinking he is about to die. Just then Stanley remembers a wintry day years earlier when he was out playing with his mother and slipped on the ice and was about to cry. But at the last moment, Stanley decided to laugh instead.

A: That was me putting myself in Stanley's shoes. I thought, *If I was about to die, I would try to think about some really strong, happy memory.* I'd rather be thinking about that than about the warden and the hot desert sun.

Q: Do you have a work routine?

A: I write every morning. For the first draft I may work just an hour a day. As I get to know the story better, I work longer

LOUIS SACHAR 187

and longer—maybe three hours. For the final draft, I'll work longer still.

Q: Why of all the characters in *Holes* did you take up Armpit's story in *Small Steps*? Why not Zero's?

A: I thought I left Stanley and Zero in a good place. I imagined that somebody like Armpit would have had a pretty tough life before he got there, and now it's going to be even worse because he missed a year of school and he's got a criminal record. So I was more interested in writing about someone like him.

Q: By the time you wrote *Small Steps*, you had already won the Newbery Medal and National Book Award for *Holes* and had worked on the film version of the book. Is that why you also wanted to write about fame?

A: Yes. After the wild ride with the movie, the thrill of being "out there," for me it was now back to taking the small steps of writing a book again. When Armpit has to decide whether to continue working for Rain Creek Irrigation digging trenches or go live the high life as a tagalong with Kyra, it was in some sense also about me leaving behind the glamour of Hollywood, me going back to work at what I do.

Q: As your daughter has gotten older, have you wanted to write about older characters?

A: That's probably another reason why I wrote about Armpit. My daughter was sixteen or seventeen when I started that book.

Q: What is the best thing about being a writer?

A: Most of the time when I'm writing it's a struggle, and there are many days when I think, *Oh, I'm never going to finish this. It's not worth finishing. There are too many flaws in it.* But when a book is going well, I'm happy. And all in all I feel that writing is very satisfying, and that I learn a lot about myself in pushing my limits to create something out of nothing.

A LOUIS SACHAR READER

The Boy Who Lost His Face (Knopf, 1989)

Dogs Don't Tell Jokes (Knopf, 1991)

Holes (Frances Foster/Farrar, Straus and Giroux, 1998)

Small Steps (Delacorte, 2006)

Someday Angeline, illustrated by Barbara Samuels
　　(Knopf, 1990)

There's a Boy in the Girls' Bathroom (Knopf, 1987)

The Wayside School books:
　　Sideways Stories from Wayside School, illustrated
　　　　by Dennis Hockerman (Follett, 1978)
　　Wayside School Is Falling Down, illustrated by Joel
　　　　Schick (Lothrop, Lee and Shepard, 1989)
　　Sideways Arithmetic from Wayside School
　　　　(Scholastic, 1989)
　　More Sideways Arithmetic from Wayside School
　　　　(Scholastic, 1994)
　　Wayside School Gets a Little Stranger, illustrated
　　　　by Joel Schick (Morrow, 1995)

JON SCIESZKA

Born 1954, Flint, Michigan

W hat's so funny, Mr. Scieszka?"

The dour fifth-grade religion teacher was sure she had finally nailed the wayward boy in the last row. And so she was not prepared when, rather than murmur a pat apology, the bright-eyed eleven-year-old launched into a side-splitting tale about an armless bell ringer who makes beautiful music by striking carillon bells with his head. ("What's that guy's name?" came the punch line at long last. "I don't know, but his face sure rings a bell.") The class's roar of approval, and the teacher's grimace, taught Jon Scieszka an unforgettable lesson about the rewards and risks of being a jokester.

Scieszka grew up in a large, raucous Midwestern family that functioned at times as a comedy school for the quietly mischievous A-student. Even so, when he moved to New York after college to study creative writing, his goal was to make his mark as an author of dark, edgy adult fiction. Comic writers whom he came to admire, as well as the experience of teaching second-graders, gradually lured him back to humor as a type of storytelling that not only came naturally to him but often also seemed the best way to say what he meant.

Scieszka first became known for the picture books—*The True Story of the Three Little Pigs* and *The Stinky Cheese Man*, among others—he created with his friends illustrator Lane Smith and designer Molly Leach. He later branched out as the author of the Time Warp Trio chapter books and as founder of the Guys Read foundation, through which he set out to show boys that reading could be just as cool—and satisfying—as video games and sports. Then, in 2008, something even more remarkable happened to the one-time class clown: the Library of Congress and the Children's Book Council named him America's first National Ambassador of Young People's Literature.

All right then, Ambassador Scieszka. What's so funny?

Leonard S. Marcus: What kind of child were you? Did you think of yourself as funny?

Jon Scieszka: Funny? Definitely. At home, being funny was a survival skill. It was a way to get some airtime at the dinner table, and to survive. With five brothers besides me, it really was like a fight for airtime—and food and water and clothing! That's why it was so good to be one of the older ones.

Q: Just saying "pass the vegetables" wasn't good enough?

A: No, you had to *get* them. My brother Jeff, the youngest one, would always end up with the chicken back. The rest of us would say, "No, that's a *big* piece. Take *that*"—and there would be nothing there but bone. My older brother Jim, who became a lawyer, was a fast talker. He would talk a mile a minute. I found that if I could tell a joke and get everyone to laugh and pause for a bit, I could then swoop in for the potatoes or the extra piece of bread.

But being funny was also about having an audience. I distinctly remember being at the dinner table and repeating some really lewd joke I had heard as a sixth-grader and getting a great laugh from all my brothers. Then came that moment when Mom and Dad were looking at me and going, "Maybe that went a little too far. . . ."

Q: "A little too far" isn't such a bad reaction from parents.

A: Both my mom and dad are pretty funny, but especially my mom. She has a snappy, fast-paced delivery. She's a nurse. Hospitals are high-intensity places where you relieve the pressure by being funny. Nurses collect some of the raunchiest jokes. One of her favorites is the one about the proctologist who is seeing a patient and looks down at his pocket and pulls out his thermometer and says, "Oh, shit, some asshole's got my pen!" We all loved that. By then I was already in high school, though the little guys were probably still in grade school. After a while, the punch line entered the Scieszka family lore. Any one of us could say "some asshole's got my pen" anytime and get a laugh at home.

Q: What about your father?

A: His sense of humor was more easygoing. He was always willing to have a laugh. As a fund-raiser, he organized games of donkey basketball at the elementary school where he was the principal. They would cover the gym floor with tarps, and guys would show up with these donkeys. They would put teachers on the donkeys and let them run around the gym and try to score baskets.

Q: That was your father's idea?

A: I think it was! At home, he taught us all to play cards and was a master of conning you in a funny way. He'd change the rules of a game by talking fast and befuddling everyone. You'd say, "Oh, the black cards aren't worth *anything* in this game? It's the *red* ones?" And he'd say, "Oh, no, *that's* what you thought?" and then he'd just scoop in the pot and say, "Let's play another round."

Q: What was your idea of a good time?

A: Watching cartoons on TV, reading *Mad* magazine. Recreating battles with my brother Jim on the floor with our elaborate collection of toy soldiers.

> The sun beat down on my hatless, un-sunscreened head. I imagined a tall, cool glass of water.
>
> "I'm starting to go crazy. And I've only been in the desert for two minutes. . . ."
>
> I tried to think calmly. What would Sam do in a situation like this? He would freak out, then remember something he read about how to survive in the desert.
>
> "What have I read about the desert? It's made of sand. It's hot. You die."
>
> *Marco? Polo!*

Looney Tunes were cartoons that were parodies of cartoons. They'd "run out of color" and suddenly switch to black and white. I knew that someone had made this thing in color, so that when they broke the convention I was in on the joke. I thought it was the funniest thing ever. They had an obnoxious character called Screwball Squirrel who talked through his nose. He would fall down the hill and out of the frame, and you'd hear this big crash. Then they would pan down the hill and you'd see that it was him playing the drums that had made that huge racket. They'd just bend your brain.

Early on, *Mad* tagged advertising as fake. We were in that first wave of products being advertised to kids, all the cereals and stuff. I remember what a disappointment that collection of battleships was that I sent away for from the back of the comic book. It had said you could get 103 battleships for ninety-eight cents. It looked so good in the picture; it was a fleet! But when they came in the mail, it was as big as a cigarette pack. We opened it and thought, *We've been had!*

Q: Was that a turning point for you?

A: I think it was! Later I got the voice of A. Wolf in *The True Story of the Three Little Pigs* from an Isuzu car commercial, with this guy who was obviously lying, promising you the world. I thought, *That's A. Wolf. He's a car salesman.*

Q: Did you play outdoors?

A: That was the best. There were always empty lots in our neighborhood with construction material and dirt piles. We'd have dirt-clod wars, dig trenches, and build elaborate forts. As we got older and could ride our bikes around, we found where some storm drains outletted into the river and would go into them and walk around under the city and see how far we could go. "Let's go meet at the black pipes," we'd say. They were big, black pipes, big enough that we could stand up in them as eight-year-olds. We never found any bodies, unfortunately. It was this great, creepy kind of adventure, hugely exciting and completely forbidden. There would be cigarette butts and beer cans left behind by the older kids who also hung out there, and some good graffiti. I remember the words "bloody tampon"— which just puzzled the hell out of me. What could that mean?

Q: Were you much of a reader?

A: Our house was packed with books. My dad didn't read to us, but he always brought books home. It was my mom who read us *Go, Dog. Go!* and *Caps for Sale* and *Mike Mulligan* and *The Five Chinese Brothers* and all the Dr. Seuss stuff. We had encyclopedias at home that I would read from cover to cover. I didn't need a lecture about reading being good. We were immersed in the stuff.

Q: What did you like about the books your mother read to you?

A: *Go, Dog. Go!* really rocked my world! It was so different from what I was reading at Catholic school, like *Fun with Dick and Jane,* which seemed so weird to me. I wondered, *Where do people act like that? Where is that part of the world?* It wasn't my house, and it wasn't any of my friends' houses, which were much more raucous kinds of places. Our house was like a gladiator preparedness school, with some feeding going on. And to see Dick and Jane walking around and talking like that, I thought, *Wow, I wonder if that's what you're supposed to do?* Then I read *Go, Dog. Go!* It was so different and somehow much saner. That and Dr. Seuss. I thought, *Now this is more like it, more like how I see the world,* even though it might be a story about a bunch of different colored dogs driving around in cars going to have a party up a tree. Somehow, that looked like our house. All those dogs in the bed? That was sort of like us. And it was funny. There are no jokes in Dick and Jane. No humor at all. Where's the "asshole got my pen" joke? The mom in Dick and Jane isn't telling that one.

Q: Were you a good student anyway?

A: I realized early on at Catholic school that being a good student had its advantages. When there would be a disturbance in the back of the classroom—it might be me, in sixth or seventh grade, telling a farmer's-daughter joke to the guy sitting next to me—the nun would look at us and say, "Who's causing the trouble back there? Scieszka's a good reader. He's OK. It was probably that friend of his."

Q: What about writing? Did that interest you then?

A: I was good at little poems, the kind of thing you would have to do in fourth, fifth grade. But I look back at the blizzard of work we did then, and it was pretty much all rote learning. I don't think we had any "creative writing" assignments. Basic math was perfect for that kind of school, because the proofs didn't lie and the numbers didn't change. There was only one answer, and either you were right or you were wrong. The red pencil either came out or it didn't.

Q: That couldn't have been much fun.

A: The nuns were either friendly and nice or mean and dangerous. I would ask in fifth-grade religion class, "What about the people who've never heard about God? They're not going to hell, are they?" And the teacher would say, "Oh, yes they are!" I got the worst grade in that class, because all I did that year was argue with her. That was a key moment for me, because I realized that I was not going to change my teacher's mind. It was also when I decided, *Well, if that's what your group's doing, I'm not with you people.* And I think that was when I learned to poke fun at the authorities, rather than to try and take them head on.

Q: It's a big thing to turn your back on a religion.

A: Yeah, but it was just that clear to me. I was also reading in the newspaper about the fighting in Ireland, and I would think, *That doesn't seem right to me: these people saying, "My God's better than your God," and then killing each other.* I had to keep going to church until high school, mainly for my father's sake. But I became an agnostic in fifth grade.

Q: From Catholic school you went on to a military academy, starting with tenth grade. That sounds like "out of the frying pan and into the fire"!

A: Apparently, I just didn't feel I'd been getting enough discipline from the nuns! Of course, at my new school we got to shoot guns.

My dad knew the public school system in Flint, Michigan, was awful, so we looked around for private schools for me to go to. Being one of six boys, money was a bit tight, and so we tried to get scholarship money. I got the most money to go to Culver Military Academy. My older brother had already gone there, and so we knew it was really good academically.

Jim thought it was fun to march around and have a sword and a gun, and I foolishly followed him down there. It was only after I arrived that it hit me, *Oh, man! You've got to march to breakfast!* We marched to breakfast, lunch, and dinner. We'd be marching to breakfast, and I'd be thinking, *Why?* After marching around for a while with one of those heavy old guns, my aspiration became to be an officer, because then I could have a sword, which was much lighter—and deadlier looking, too. And so I became Lieutenant Scieszka.

Q: It sounds like you came to like it there.

A: It was a spectacular place to learn. That's where I got interested in math and science. One of my math teachers, an older

Lieutenant John Scieszka as a high-school senior, 1972

man with white hair who we thought was a hundred, had such a playful, breezy understanding of math. He could sit at his desk with his back to the blackboard and write algebraic equations upside down and backwards. He was a really tall guy, and he'd just grab the chalk and start writing flawless equations behind his back. It was quite a show, and we'd all sit there and think, *We can't even figure this stuff out forward!* I later noticed that mathematicians tend to be good joke tellers, and I think that's because humor is mathematical. A joke will often start out as an expected progression. It takes you through the progression to a certain point, but then instead of going for the conclusion it's been leading up to, the joke will jump off to the side or make some surprise leap. It's all about expectation, and you have to have the mathematical talent to get there.

We also had an amazing library at school. I wandered around in the stacks one day and found Kafka's *The Trial*, this dusty little black book that hadn't been checked out in years. I thought, *I'm the* first *guy to have read* The Trial. *I am so cool.* And the book so spoke to me, maybe because school itself was in some ways like *The Trial*, such a weird bureaucracy. Just like Catholic school, it was a kind of double world, where you had to keep your sense of humor in check or otherwise the authorities would kill you. ROTC class was kind of like fifth-grade religion class all over again, where with a straight face people would be teaching us things like how to set up a Claymore mine and lay a nice field of fire. I had a friend in the class, a guy from Boulder who was an out-and-out hippie. We would sit in the back and say to each other, "Did he just say that? Is he telling us how to kill people?" Everybody else was furiously writing down notes! We got in a lot of trouble in that class. Our teacher was a war vet and a real dude, the classic hard-talking sergeant with the funny haircut. He would always say, "Scieszka. Spellman. You better straighten up and fly right!" One day he put on a movie, and just as he turned off the lights we unhooked the take-up reel, so that it fed out into a pile on the floor. When he turned on the lights, there was this massive pile of film on the floor. We tried not to laugh, but I think he saw us. That is how I survived doing something as weird as marching to breakfast in the rain with fifty guys dressed exactly like me at six thirty in the morning in Indiana. I had to make a joke out of it.

Q: In college and graduate school, you got serious about being a writer. Maybe even a little too serious?

A: I was being fueled by all those dark Germanic writers, the darker the better—Kafka, Thomas Mann, Günter Grass. I wanted to be a suffering artist! Once I got to the graduate writing program at Columbia, I found that the people I liked were the funny guys. One of the students was writing hilarious stuff. My stuff started to get funnier too. I got away from my brooding, jump-off-the-bridge kind of writing and thought, *Yeah, it should be funny.*

Q: How did you get from that to teaching and writing for kids?

A: It was surprisingly easy. After I got out of school, I was painting apartments to pay the rent, crawling around bathrooms in New York in August with a can of paint, and I thought, *I've got to do something else.* I heard about a teaching job. When they hired me I was still kind of oblivious. I was thinking, *I've been*

> I take the milk out for my cereal and wonder:
> 1. How many quarts in a gallon?
> 2. How many pints in a quart?
> 3. How many inches in a foot?
> 4. How many feet in a yard?
> 5. How many yards in a neighborhood? How many inches in a pint? How many feet in my shoes?
>
> *Math Curse*

a kid. My dad was a teacher. I can teach kids. Teaching second grade and reading to the kids is how I found the really crucial piece about children's books, which is that the best children's books are those that you can read aloud. *The Phantom Tollbooth.* The Frog and Toad books. *George and Martha.* I read those stories so many times to my class, and they were still hilarious. Then it hit me. This is what *I* should be doing. So I took a year off to do nothing but write.

Q: You taught kids of several different grades. Did their idea of what was funny vary much from grade to grade?

A: Absolutely. What's funny to a preschooler is just stupid to a first-grader, and it's the same from first to second grade. Second grade is a key age, because it's when they've just become readers and feel they've figured out the world. They think, *Here are all the rules.* That's why second-graders love parody, and why I love writing for them, taking a form and twisting it or layering in onto a different subject matter—doing poetry for science or doing a funny math book. I love that weird collision of form and content, and so do they.

Some kids don't get parody and really can't stand it. It just seems wrong to them. Adults who don't "get the joke" can have some pretty extreme reactions too. When people don't enjoy someone's humor, they will respond with panic, sometimes even with fear. It's almost like you've attacked them. You've attacked their integrity. They may decide that something must be wrong with you if you think it's funny. They may even take their crusade out to other people and say that other people should not find it funny either.

But it was because of that second-grade love of parody that

I've had kids write to me about the endpapers in *The Stinky Cheese Man*. The endpapers—but it's not the end! That is the funniest thing in the book for them. I'm hoping to be their *Go, Dog. Go!* And then they'll explain it to me, *why* having the endpapers come early is so funny. They'll actually write about that in the letter, because they want to let me know they got the joke.

The weirder kinds of humor take an older kid. Like the humor in *Squids Will Be Squids* is almost absurdist, with punch lines that are hard to explain. The morals are sort of non sequiturs. It throws some kids for a loop. Kids either love that book or don't get it.

Q: Do you think there is such a thing as boy humor and girl humor?

A: Yes. It sounds stereotypical, but it's the boys who go for that broader, slapsticky, Three Stooges humor. I've met only one woman who said she liked *The Three Stooges*. My mom would come in and say, "*What* are you watching?" We would be hysterical, on the floor, laughing. It wasn't that we were going to poke each other in the eye ourselves—not exactly, anyway. We wouldn't actually take the crowbar and put it up our little brother's nose. But it seemed so darn funny to see them do it. Captain Underpants is a great example of a series that second- and third-grade boys are just passionate about. They are the funniest books they have ever read. But there are teachers who think those books are evil.

Q: What happened to your sense of humor after 9/11? Some comic writers and comedians stopped working.

A: I did too for a while. I thought, *What is the point?* The thing

CHAPTER II

But before the Black Knight arrives, maybe I should explain how three regular guys happened to find themselves facing death by shish-ka-bob.

It all started at my birthday party. My two best friends, Fred and Sam were over at my house. We were just sitting around the kitchen table doing birthday kind of things. You know--- eating junk, drinking soda, ~~and opening presents. And that's how we got into this whole mess, honest~~. *looking at the baseball my sister had given to me*

~~My mom and dad gave me the basketball I wanted. My goofball sister actually got me a nice fishing pole. And my grandma sent me a grandma kind of sweater. Like I said, just the regular birthday kind of stuff.~~

My mom started scooping up wrapping paper to throw away.

That's when Sam found the *other* present.

"Hey Joe, here's one you missed." Sam held up a ~~present about the size of a telephone book~~ *small rectangular present.* It was wrapped in black *and gold* paper, ~~with small gold stars and moons all over it.~~

"Who's it from?"

My mom read the card and made a sour face. "Your Uncle Joe."

"Yahoo!"

Uncle Joe was the best uncle anybody could have. He was a

Manuscript page from *The Knights of the Kitchen Table*

that got me started again was reading to kids and hearing from kids. They showed me that we still need funny books. That's what makes me think that humor is such a basic part of being a human being. It was the response that got people going again.

Q: Your Time Warp Trio book about the Brooklyn Bridge came out the following year.

A: I had started writing *Hey Kid, Want to Buy a Bridge?* before 9/11, and I found that I had to change some of the wording afterward, before it was published. In the first chapter I had originally had the boys standing by the end of the unfinished bridge. Joe, looking out at the landscape of lower Manhattan, sees that there are no Twin Towers and decides that the three of them must have traveled way into the future, where everything's gone all crazy, as in some futuristic disaster movie. After 9/11, I thought, *I can't say that now.* So in the final version, the kids say something like, "Something weird happened to Manhattan. It's all so little." Then they realize that they are not in the future, but in the past, and that that's why there are no Twin Towers. They haven't been built yet.

Q: Empires come and go, but life always goes on in those books.

A: That's the one thing I hope kids take from the Time Warp books, that there have been civilizations before us that went on way longer and figured out a lot of things way better than we have. The Mayans had a better calendar than ours, thousands of years ago. They were better at math. We always think, *We're the best. We're making these giant trucks!* We may be the pinnacle of civilization in some ways, but in other ways we just aren't.

Q: How do you go about writing the Time Warp books? Do you do much research?

A: They take a ton of research. I start by trying to find an era that I'm interested in. I'd known about the Mayans' numbering system and their astronomy, but meanwhile they were also an incredibly brutal culture, ripping people's hearts out. I thought, *Great!* The Time Warp kids always have to go someplace where there's great weaponry. I've never sent them to a war, though. I tried getting them to the Civil War, but it just seemed so wrong. What do you do? Have them lose a leg? A lot of the research involves finding just the right historical moment, when people and events came together. For the Brooklyn Bridge book, it was the moment when the bridge was going up and Thomas Edison had his laboratory across the river in New Jersey and might very well have run into the bridge's designer, John Roebling. I make sure that everything is historically accurate, except for the part about three guys able to travel through time. I see these three fourth- or fifth-grade boys as not being awed by anything. "Mr. Edison, can you make a spark? Make a bigger one! Can you set anything on fire?" Their take on the world is, "Can we get something to eat?"

Q: Do you do revise your work much?

A: Reading my stuff out loud to kids is a big part of it. That's the acid test. Humor is less forgiving than other kinds of writing. You're so dependent on the rhythm and the punch line. After I read the stories in *The Stinky Cheese Man* to kids at a lot of schools, they ended up maybe half as long as they started out. They got shorter and shorter and more to the point.

I worked at trying to do a funny math book for maybe five years. I would work on it, put it away, try again, put it away. I try to explain that to kids, but I think they think that I'm kidding. I could not figure out the form. Then when I thought of those awful word problems we had to do in school, it just fell into place.

Q: What do you like best about writing for young people?

A: I think it goes back to being in fifth grade: telling the joke to get the laugh. It's something about making people laugh, either right away with an audience, or later when a kid writes to me and I hear about it. I got a letter from a boy once who wrote, "I read *Science Curse* and I laughed so hard buggers flew out of my nose and I fell off my chair." It was all brutally misspelled, which made it even funnier for me. I sat there picturing this little guy, and I thought, *My God, how good is that?*

A JON SCIESZKA READER

Cowboy and Octopus, illustrated by Lane Smith
(Viking, 2007)
An autobiography:
*Knucklehead: Tall Tales & Mostly True Stories
About Growing Up Scieszka* (Viking, 2008)
Math Curse, illustrated by Lane Smith (Viking, 1995)

Science Verse, illustrated by Lane Smith (Viking, 2004)

Squids Will Be Squids: Fresh Morals for Beastly Fables,
    illustrated by Lane Smith (Viking, 1998)

The Stinky Cheese Man, illustrated by Lane Smith (Viking,
    1992)

The Time Warp Trio books:

> *The Knights of the Kitchen Table,* illustrated by Lane
>   Smith (Viking, 1991)
>
> *The Not-So-Jolly Roger,* illustrated by Lane Smith
>   (Viking, 1991)
>
> *The Good, the Bad, and the Goofy,* illustrated by Lane
>   Smith (Viking, 1992)
>
> *Your Mother Was a Neanderthal,* illustrated by Lane
>   Smith (Viking, 1993)
>
> *2095,* illustrated by Lane Smith (Viking, 1995)
>
> *Tut, Tut,* illustrated by Lane Smith (Viking, 1996)
>
> *Sam Samurai,* illustrated by Lane Smith (Viking, 2001)
>
> *Hey Kid, Want to Buy a Bridge?,* illustrated by Adam
>   McCauley (Viking, 2002)
>
> *Marco? Polo!,* illustrated by Adam McCauley (Viking,
>   2006)

The True Story of the Three Little Pigs by A. Wolf, as told to
    Jon Scieszka, illustrated by Lane Smith (Viking, 1989)

ACKNOWLEDGMENTS

I wish to express my thanks to the writers who took part in the making of *Funny Business.* I am grateful for the time and thought they gave to this project as well as for their generosity in lending photographs, manuscript pages, and other illustration materials for reproduction in these pages.

I would also like to express my appreciation to the following individuals for their help with arranging for the loan and use of illustrations, with fact-checking, and with related matters: Laura Arnold, Katie Browning, Kay Curtis, Elizabeth Daniel, Sigrid Estrada, Lila Haber, Perry Hagopian, Jeri Hansen, Lucy Ingrams, Amanda Johnson, Jeanne Juster, Christine Labov, Barbara Lalicki, Fritha Lindqvist, Penny Luithlen, Jeanne McLellan, Margaret Miller, Philippa Mills, Emily D. Pardo, Sarah Payne, Susan Rich, Lyle Rigg, Dina Sherman, Joan Slattery, Darla Spiers, Saundra B. Taylor, Amanda F. Vega, Deborah Wakefield, Kate Webster, Karen Wojtyla, and Allison Wortche.

I thank my editors, Elizabeth Bicknell and Kaylan Adair, designer Sherry Fatla, and my agent, George M. Nicholson, for their thoughtful guidance, careful attention to detail, and good fellowship at every turn. And thanks as always to my wife, Amy, and our son, Jacob, for their love, support, and laughter.

Photography Credits and Copyright Acknowledgments

Index